Please check all items for damages
before leaving the Library.
Thereafter you will be held
responsible for all injuries
to items beyond reasonable wear.

10   4/12

10   10/13

FEB - - 1995

THE OLD MAN AND THE SEA

Story of a Common Man

TWAYNE'S MASTERWORK STUDIES

Robert Lecker, General Editor

THE OLD MAN AND THE SEA

Story of a Common Man

Gerry Brenner

TWAYNE PUBLISHERS • NEW YORK
Maxwell Macmillan Canada • Toronto
Maxwell Macmillan International • New York   Oxford   Singapore   Sydney

813.09
HEM

Twayne's Masterwork Studies No. 80

Twayne Publishers   Maxwell Macmillan Canada, Inc.
Macmillan Publishing Company   1200 Eglinton Avenue East
866 Third Avenue   Suite 200
New York, New York 10022   Don Mills, Ontario M3C 3N1

Macmillan Publishing Company is part of the Maxwell Communication
Group of Companies.

Library of Congress Cataloging-in-Publication Data

Brenner, Gerry, 1937–
    The old man and the sea : story of a common man / Gerry Brenner.
        p.   cm. — (Twayne's masterwork studies ; no. 80)
    Includes bibliographical references and index.
        ISBN 0-8057-7991-4. — ISBN 0-8057-8040-8 (pbk.)
        1. Hemingway, Ernest, 1899–1961. Old man and the sea. I. Title.
    II. Series.
    PS3515.E370515   1991
    813'.52—dc20   91-20136

The paper used in this publication meets the minimum requirements
of American National Standard for Information Sciences—Permanence
of Paper for Printed Library Materials, ANSI Z39.48-1984. ⊗™

10 9 8 7 6 5 4 3 2 1 (hc)
10 9 8 7 6 5 4 3 2 1 (pb)

Copyediting supervised by Barbara Sutton.
Book production by Janet Z. Reynolds.
Typeset by World Composition Services, Inc., Sterling, Virginia.

Printed in the United States of America.

Contents

Note on the References and Acknowledgments

The text to which I refer in this book is the standard 127-page Scribner Library paperback edition (New York: Charles Scribner's Sons, 1952). All parenthetical page references are to this edition.

For permission to quote from Ernest Hemingway's works, I gratefully acknowledge Macmillan Publishing Co.: *Death in the Afternoon*, copyright 1932 by Charles Scribner's Sons, renewed 1960 by Ernest Hemingway; *The Old Man and the Sea*, copyright 1952 by Ernest Hemingway; renewed 1980 by Mary Hemingway; *By-Line: Ernest Hemingway*, © 1967 by Mary Hemingway.

For permission to use again his 1953 photograph of Ernest Hemingway for the frontispiece, I thank photographer Ted Sato and John Arden of the John and Mabel Ringling Museum of Art; the photograph originally appeared in the 1953 *Ringling Brothers and Barnum and Bailey Circus Magazine*. For permission to use the photographs of Ernest Hemingway with marlin catches, early and late, I thank the Ernest Hemingway Foundation and Allan B. Goodrich, Supervisory Archivist of Boston's John Fitzgerald Kennedy Library.

For their patience I wish to thank Robert Lecker, general editor of this series, and Lewis DeSimone, Twayne editor. Other writing commitments kept me from prompt completion of this study, and I have appreciated the tolerance and generous deadline extensions these men permitted me. Special thanks are due Barbara Sutton for a fine job of copyediting a wordy manuscript and the many students at the University of Montana who have discussed with open-minded goodwill and intellectual integrity the complex issues in Hemingway's little novel. Once again I thank my wife, Terry, for listening to and challenging much of what appears here; her confidence, support, understanding, and love have, as before, sustained me in my efforts.

Chronology:
Ernest Hemingway's Life and Works

1896	Clarence Edmonds "Ed" Hemingway—physician, naturalist, and disciplinarian—weds Grace Hall—concert-quality contralto, voice teacher, and Congregationalist—in Oak Park, a Chicago suburb, 1 October.
1898	Marcelline Hemingway born 15 January.
1899	Ernest Miller Hemingway born 21 July.
1900	Family begins annual summerings in Windemere Cottage at Walloon Lake on the Michigan peninsula.
1901	Ernest utters first complete sentence on St. Patrick's Day: "I don't know Buffalo Bill."
1902	Ursula Hemingway born 29 April.
1903	Ernest receives birthday present of all-day fishing trip with father.
1904	Madelaine "Sunny" Hemingway born 28 November.
1905	Ernest begins first grade with Marcelline at Holmes Grammar School; she is held back a year to promote Grace's plan to raise them as "twins."
1906	Family moves into Oak Park home designed by Grace at 600 North Kenilworth Avenue.
1910	Vacations with his mother on Nantucket Island and hears tales of his seafaring great-grandfather, Alexander Hancock.
1911	Writes first story as a sixth-grade exercise, "My First Sea Vouge" [Voyage], drawn from Nantucket vacation. Carol Hemingway born 19 July. Receives single-barrel, 20-gauge shotgun as birthday gift from grandfather Anson Hemingway.
1913–1917	Attends Oak Park and River Forest Township High School where he writes for the school newspaper and literary maga-

zine, plays cello in the school orchestra, captains the water-basketball squad, swims on the swim team, and letters as a second-stringer on the football team.

1915   Leicester Clarence Hemingway born 1 April.

1917   Ernest graduates from high school as "Class Prophet" for his literary achievements. Spurns college. Moves to Kansas City and in October begins a six-month stint as cub reporter for the *Star*.

1918   Disqualified from joining the regular armed forces because of his genetically weak left eye, joins the Italian Red Cross ambulance corps. Wounded in both legs by trench mortar 8 July. Recuperates in Red Cross Hospital in Milan, Italy, and falls in love with nurse Agnes Von Kurowsky.

1919   Returns to Oak Park as injured war hero. Is rejected by Agnes. Begins writing fiction.

1920   Moves to Toronto and writes human-interest news stories for the *Toronto Star Weekly*. Moves to Chicago. Meets poet Carl Sandburg and fiction writer Sherwood Anderson. Continues writing fiction. Begins dating 28-year-old Hadley Richardson.

1921   Marries Hadley 3 September. Agrees to write features part time as European correspondent for the *Toronto Star Weekly*. Sails with Hadley for Paris 8 December.

1922   In Paris, Hemingways set up house in Latin Quarter. Meets writers Gertrude Stein, Ezra Pound, John Dos Passos, James Joyce, and Ford Madox Ford. Covers the Greco-Turkish War in Constantinople and conferences in Geneva and Lausanne. In December, Hadley leaves Paris to join Ernest in Lausanne; the valise containing nearly all of Ernest's manuscripts gets stolen.

1923   Travels to Spain to see bullfights for first time. Contact Editions publishes *Three Stories and Ten Poems*. Returns with Hadley to Toronto for birth of John Hadley "Bumby" Nicanor Hemingway, 10 October.

1924   Three Mountains Press publishes *in our time*. Hemingways return to Paris. Becomes associate editor of Ford Madox Ford's *transatlantic review* and enlarges his circle of literary friends.

1925   Boni and Liveright publishes *In Our Time*. Meets Pauline Pfeiffer, staff worker for the Paris edition of *Vogue* magazine, and author F. Scott Fitzgerald. Returns with Hadley and friends to Pamplona, which gives him basis for beginning *The Sun Also*

Rises. Writes *The Torrents of Spring*, a satire on Boni and Liveright's leading author, Sherwood Anderson. Hemingways spend second winter in Schruns; joined for the holidays by Pauline Pfeiffer.

1926   Boni and Liveright rejects *Torrents*, prompting contract with Scribners, which publishes it and *The Sun Also Rises*. In love with Pauline Pfeiffer, separates from Hadley in August; divorce proceedings begin in November.

1927   Marries Pauline 10 May in Paris. Summer spent in Spain; attends the Pamplona festival for fifth consecutive year. *Men without Women* (short stories) published.

1928   Begins writing *A Farewell to Arms*. Moves to Key West, Florida; begins ocean fishing. Patrick Hemingway born by caesarean section 28 June in Kansas City, Missouri. Ernest's father commits suicide 6 December.

1929   *A Farewell to Arms* published.

1930   Begins writing *Death in the Afternoon*, aesthetic treatise on bullfighting. Hospitalized eight weeks in Billings, Montana, after breaking arm in car wreck in October.

1931   Pauline's uncle buys Key West home as gift for her. Gregory Hancock Hemingway born by caesarean section 12 November in Kansas City.

1932   Takes two-month fishing expedition to Havana and begins marlin fishing. *Death in the Afternoon* published.

1933   New men's magazine publishes "Marlin Off the Morro," the first of 25 "*Esquire* Letters." Fishing near Cuba, catches 50 marlin in two months. Publishes third story collection, *Winner Take Nothing*. Sails with Pauline to Paris, then to Africa for a safari in Kenya and Tanganyika.

1934   Starts *Green Hills of Africa*, fictionalized account of a safari.

1935   Publishes *Green Hills of Africa*.

1936   Publishes "The Snows of Kilimanjaro" and "The Short Happy Life of Francis Macomber." Completes the "Harry Morgan stories" for *To Have and Have Not*. Meets journalist Martha Gellhorn.

1937   Covers Spanish Civil War as correspondent for North American Newspaper Alliance. Begins affair with Martha Gellhorn. Publishes *To Have and Have Not*. Writes only play, *The Fifth Column*.

1938	Shuttles between Spain and the United States. Writes antifascist articles for *Ken* magazine. Publishes *The Fifth Column and the First Forty-nine Stories*.
1939	Moves to Cuba with Martha Gellhorn, preparing Finca Vigía (Lookout Farm) outside Havana for residence. Begins *For Whom the Bell Tolls*. Makes first visit to Sun Valley, Idaho.
1940	Publishes *For Whom the Bell Tolls*. Divorced from Pauline 14 November; marries Martha Gellhorn 21 November in Cheyenne, Wyoming.
1941	Hemingways spend six months in China. Pulitzer Prize Fiction Committee unanimously selects *For Whom the Bell Tolls*; board chairman vetoes selection; no prize for fiction awarded that year.
1942	Runs U.S. Embassy–approved counterintelligence organization to thwart Nazi infiltration into Cuba; patrols north coast of Cuba for Nazi submarines aboard his fishing boat, *Pilar*. Edits *Men at War*, anthology of stories and historical accounts of war.
1943	Marital discord; Martha leaves for Europe as war correspondent for *Collier's* magazine.
1944	Hired as war correspondent for *Collier's*. In London, meets Mary Welsh, married writer for the London bureaus of *Time*, *Life*, and *Fortune* magazines. Covers war with U.S. Fourth Infantry.
1945	Returns to Cuba; Mary Welsh joins him at the Finca Vigía in May. Mary obtains divorce. Martha Gellhorn's divorce from Hemingway is final 21 December.
1946	Marries Mary Welsh in Havana 14 March. Works on *The Garden of Eden*. En route to Sun Valley, rescues Mary from the brink of death when a tubular pregnancy ruptures.
1947	Begins to have blood pressure problems. Receives Bronze Star for war information work. Drafts the "Bimini" section of *Islands in the Stream*.
1948	Travels in Italy, visiting favorite places. Becomes enamored of 18-year-old Adriana Ivancich.
1949	Writing *Across the River and into the Trees*.
1950	*The New Yorker* publishes Lillian Ross's notorious profile of Hemingway. Scribners publishes *Across the River and into the Trees*. Physical ailments mount.

Chronology

1951	Writes *The Old Man and the Sea*. Writes the "At Sea" section of *Islands in the Stream*. Deaths of mother 28 June and Pauline Pfeiffer 2 October.
1952	*Life* magazine publishes *The Old Man and the Sea* 1 September.
1953	Wins Pulitzer Prize for *The Old Man and the Sea*. Spends summer in Spain, following the bullfights for first time since 1930. Travels to Africa for a five-month safari.
1954	Leaving Africa, crashes in two successive flights; suffers serious burns and a concussion; his death reported by international press. Awarded Nobel Prize for Literature, but poor health prevents him from attending awards ceremony in Stockholm.
1955	Begins *African Journal*, nonfiction account of recent safari. Assists in filming *The Old Man and the Sea*. Continues to suffer from health problems.
1956	Spends month in Peru for filming of *The Old Man and the Sea*. Spends fall following bullfights in Spain and winter in Paris.
1957	Returns to Cuba, depressed about health. Writes *A Moveable Feast*, memoir of Paris in the early 1920s.
1958	Works on *The Garden of Eden*. Spends autumn and winter in Idaho.
1959	Buys home in Ketchum, Idaho. Returns to Spain to follow a five-month bullfighting "duel."
1960	Begins *The Dangerous Summer*, nonfiction account of bull-fighting "duel." Flies to Spain to follow bullfighting. Suffers from bouts of depression and paranoia. *Life* magazine serializes an edited version of *The Dangerous Summer*. Admitted to the Mayo Clinic in Rochester, Minnesota, for electroshock therapy.
1961	In late January, returns to Ketchum; suffers suicidal depression, leading to local hospitalizations. In April, readmitted to Mayo Clinic for two months and returns to Ketchum 30 June. Commits suicide by shotgun 2 July.

Ernest Hemingway (1899–1961) in 1953. *Photograph courtesy of Ted Sato and the John and Mabel Ringling Museum of Art*

LITERARY AND
HISTORICAL CONTEXT

1

Sketch of a Decade, 1945–1955

Part of the long-standing appeal of *The Old Man and the Sea* lies in its remoteness from our world. The story ignores events contemporary with its composition, publication, or reception[1]—the shaky political power of Cuban president Carlos Prío Socarrás at the half century, the overthrow of Prío's government in 1952 by longtime Cuban dictator and U.S.-supported ex-president Fulgencio Batista, or Fidel Castro's revolution of 26 July 1953. Such matters seem continents away from Santiago's little fishing village.

During the cool early mornings of January 1951 Ernest Hemingway was diligently drafting the novel at the Finca Vigiá, his home on the outskirts of Havana. As the world settled into the Cold War, U.S. troops were repulsing the Red Chinese in Korea with a counterattack that would drive the North Korean forces back across the thirty-eighth parallel into their own territory. And President Harry S. Truman soon would relieve General Douglas A. MacArthur as commander in chief of the United Nations Command in Korea. In this crisis-driven world Hemingway was crafting the serene novella that would bring him a Pulitzer Prize in 1953 and contribute to his Nobel Prize for Literature in 1954.

The Korean War, which broke out in late June 1950, seemed inconceivable five years earlier when President Truman brought World War II to an end by ordering the dropping of the atomic bomb on Hiroshima and Nagasaki. Instead of world peace, however, the war's end soon led to the Cold War between the United States and the Soviet Union, whose communist aggressions were felt to pose threats to political stability around the globe.

Under Truman the United States abandoned its long-standing policy of isolationism and developed a policy of containment to deal with aggressive Soviet expansionism. Truman supported various international efforts: the formation of the United Nations; the Truman Doctrine of 1947, which offered military aid to governments such as Greece and Turkey to resist subjugation by armed minorities or outside pressures; the Marshall Plan of 1948, which integrated financial aid to the nations of Western Europe for rebuilding economies and governments; the airlift of supplies into Berlin, despite Stalin's blockade; and the North Atlantic Treaty Organization (NATO), the mutual defense pact formed to protect Western nations against communist aggression.

When the Soviet Union detonated an atomic bomb late in the summer of 1949, Truman directed the Atomic Energy Commission to "continue work on all forms of atomic weapons." On 1 November 1952—two months after *The Old Man and the Sea* saw print in *Life* magazine and a few days before ex-General Dwight D. Eisenhower defeated Illinois Governor Adlai E. Stevenson in a landslide presidential election—the first hydrogen bomb was detonated on the Eniwetok atoll in the Marshall Islands: the fire ball raged five miles high and four wide; the mushroom cloud, 25 miles high and 100 wide.

On 9 February 1951 Hemingway was generating manuscript for *Old Man* at a good rate and wrote to a book reviewer that he was writing a thousand words a day—double his normal output. Exactly a year earlier the Republican senator from Wisconsin, Joseph R. McCarthy, spoke to the Ohio County Women's Republican Club in Wheeling, West Virginia, and claimed that he had in his hand a list of 205 names of Communist party members who were employed by the

4

U.S. State Department, even though their names and affiliation had been revealed to Secretary of State Dean Acheson. McCarthy's speech ignited a Red Scare that lasted four years as he subpoenaed a multitude of suspected communist sympathizers or "fellow travelers."

As Americans were experiencing the global worries of the Cold War and the Korean War, they were also focusing on the rapid changes in their domestic lives. After the war the G.I. bill gave former servicemen the financial assistance they needed to attend college and begin businesses. The Veterans Administration and the Federal Housing Administration helped finance tract homes and the suburbias that sprawled outward from big cities, dragging shopping malls, supermarkets, and service stations in their wakes.

The U.S. population increased from 2.6 million in 1940, to 3.6 million in 1950, to a peak of 4.3 million in 1957. In 1950 Americans rented two-bedroom duplexes for $92 a month, bought one of the 2 million new homes for between $8,000 and $12,000, averaged salaries of between $4,000 and $8,000, earned a minimum federal wage of 75¢ an hour, and brought home industrial-worker weekly paychecks of $60.50. Between 1945 and 1955 many Americans abandoned their farms and moved to suburbs and to the Southwest, especially to California, and they spent millions of dollars on casual clothing, discovered frozen orange juice, bought 6.7 million automobiles (a 1950 Ford cost between $1,329 and $2,262), and drove on new federally financed highways that ribboned the nation's landscape. Americans posted letters with a 3¢ stamp, bought Cokes and Snickers bars for a nickel, selected sugar-coated cold cereals from store shelves, drank 25-proof Hadacol as a health restorative, brushed their teeth with chlorophyll-added Chlorodent, and still filled fountain pens with ink.

But by the time Hemingway was preparing *Old Man* for publication in *Life* on 1 September 1952, Americans were slowly awakening to irregularities on their domestic landscape. That year 400,000 children appeared in juvenile courts on delinquency charges, a 45 percent increase in five years. In that same period the crime rate jumped 50 percent, outstripping the increase in population by four to one. Millions of Americans were living in poverty: between 20 and 25 percent of the population earned less than $3,000 annually for a family of four, or less than $4,000 for a family of six, and another 10 percent struggled to keep poverty at bay. Nevertheless, economists applauded the benefits of American capitalism—the low unemployment rate (4.6 percent), the steady rise in real wages, the low rate of inflation (1.5 percent), and the annual growth rate (4.3 percent).

Despite Truman's desegregation of the armed forces and his advocacy of the Fair Employment Practices Bill in 1946, 1950, and 1952, he failed to secure civil rights for the 16 million African Americans in the United States. This minority still lacked political power and well-paying jobs. Economically deprived and discriminated against, the 68 percent of African Americans who lived in the South also encountered legislated segregation. Instrumental in turning the tide of racism was the Reverend Oliver Brown, who, in late 1951, brought suit against the school authorities in Topeka, Kansas, for their refusal to allow him to enroll his fourth-grade daughter in all-white Sumner School, four blocks from her home, and their requirement that she attend the all-black school five miles away. The case, *Brown* v. *the Board of Education*, reached the U.S. Supreme Court, which unanimously ruled unconstitutional the "separate but equal" standard by which African Americans had long been discriminated against. Despite President Eisenhower's disapproval of the court's decision (and his regret at having appointed Earl Warren as chief justice—"the biggest damfool mistake I ever made"), despite the eruption of White Citizens' Councils in the South, despite segregationists' militant defiance of the Supreme Court's decision, and despite the backlash that saw Southern congressional representatives introduce 53 bills to slow or sidestep desegregation in the ensuing decade, Jim Crow laws were repealed and laws mandating desegregation were passed and enforced.

Between the beginning of the decade and the winter of 1952, when Hemingway was receiving the universally enthusiastic reviews of his novella of heroism, Americans were becoming television addicts. As of early 1950 only 10 percent of the U.S. populace owned a television set, and 38 percent had never seen a television program, but Americans bought 4.4 million sets in that year—a huge increase over the 7,000 sets bought four years earlier. Besides conventional entertainment fare, television let Americans watch and weep in April 1951 as General MacArthur delivered his 34-minute, old-soldiers-never-die speech before a joint session of Congress and on 23 September 1952 as vice presidential candidate Richard M. Nixon rescued his political career with a shrewdly maudlin speech in which he not only defended himself against charges that a millionaires' club had set up a secret slush fund for his private use but also declared that he would keep one anonymous gift, the cocker spaniel that gave the speech its name, Checkers.

Remote though Santiago's world is from global events at midcentury or at century's end, his final days eloquently portray a complex human—as an elderly citizen struggling to maintain self-esteem, as a role model to an increasing population of fatherless youths who seek meaningful lives, and as a confused person whose values, beliefs, and behavior are deeply problematic. Santiago's injured and exhausted body foreshadows Hemingway's final decade, when physical ailments and poor health prevent him from journeying to Stockholm to receive the Nobel Prize for Literature in December 1954. The timeless quality of *The Old Man and the Sea* also contributes to the work's stature as a masterpiece, for it makes Santiago's story meaningful to readers of different ages, cultures, and backgrounds: it speaks, and will continue to speak, across time and space.

2

The Importance of the Work

Few literary critics today regard *The Old Man and the Sea* as a masterwork, yet it appears on thousands of high school reading lists. On its surface it is a sanitary text and highly suitable for impressionable teenagers to read: its events lack sexual content; its violence is ennobled by being linked to fishing or self-protection; its sentimentalized old fisherman appears to raise few questionable moral issues; its artistic simplicity makes its grand theme of man's struggle against the forces of nature readily accessible to a wide audience; and its narrative invites simple moralizing, easy symbolic equations, and tidy Christian parallels.

If the novella is fare for only teenage readers, however, then it fails to meet two criteria required of every masterwork—to speak across historical periods to a broad range of readers and to engage readers emotionally and intellectually with its complex treatment of recurrent human issues whose significance readers can measure against the yardsticks of their own daily existence. The major portion of this study addresses the second of these criteria, but a survey of how the novella satisfies the first criterion (even though it is too early to determine whether it will speak across historical periods) should readily justify a continued reading and study of the novella—beyond the high school classroom.

Narratives often fit into a category of fable, fantasy, or fiction. A fable illustrates a moral, proves a point, or teaches an idea; a fantasy gratifies or expresses a conscious or unconscious wish or anxiety; a fiction holds up a mirror to reality to convey an experience that, or portray a character who, closely replicates actual life. Some writers' narratives routinely fall into one of these categories—for example, William Golding's fables, Franz Kafka's fantasies, and D. H. Lawrence's fictions. Most narratives resist easy slotting and tend to overlap categories. Such is the case with *Old Man*, a text that examines a person who experiences trials and tests, that invites us to find meaning in his experience, and that challenges us to assign our significance to that meaning—or to different meanings.

FABLE

Old Man has one ingredient common to all variations of the fable—the moral tag, a pithy sentence that underscores the imbedded message of the narrative. Readers can listen to Santiago's repeated self-admonishment, "Don't go too far out," and either accept or scorn parental cautions not to trespass conventional behavior and safe norms. They can also conclude that those who persevere in times of trial and keep their faith under duress will receive their due rewards or that resourcefulness sometimes leads to the sin of pride. Readers can even accept the equations that *Life*'s editorial staff offered in a preface to the magazine publication of the novella: Santiago is the aged author Hemingway, the marlin is his noble and beautiful works, and the sharks are the predatory critics and reviewers who mutilate his work and reputation. Other allegorists may see the narrative as a Western saga of humanity's recurrent battle against natural forces that test personal worth and validate the right to existence; or as Everyman's struggle with the Female Principle, as embodied in the sea and its agents; or, finally, as a psychological battle within a self-contradictory human whose actions reveal noble and ignoble impulses. As fraternal fisherman Santiago is Brother's Keeper to the marlin he repeatedly calls his brother, but as the marlin's killer Santiago is Cain the fratricide, who here exhibits the carcass of the mutilated marlin to prove his own prowess to villagers who regarded him a luckless has-been.

FANTASY

The wishes and anxieties that undergird fantasy are evident in the text's portrayal of lengthy combat between a puny man and an oversized fish. The confrontation shares the gigantism common to frontier tall tales (Davy Crockett wrestling with huge crocodiles and Pecos Bill taming a 30-foot-tall grizzly bear for his horse) and fairy tales (thimble-sized Tom Thumb swaggering his way through ordinary events, and Jack in the Beanstalk slaying a giant ogre). Such exaggeration satisfies the conventional human wish to perform in larger-than-life ways in an encounter with a colossal opponent or against seemingly insurmountable odds. Santiago's capacity to subdue an 18-foot marlin and lash it to the side of a 16-foot skiff feeds our imaginative capacity to wonder, marvel, and be awed—a primary virtue of all fairy tales.

Likewise, Santiago's exploits call to mind the mythic adventures of Jonah, David and Goliath, Prometheus, Perseus, Tristan, Beowulf, St. George, Gawain, Gilgamesh, King Kong, and various contemporary intergalactic heroes. In all of these tales a person grapples with outsized adversaries ranging from animals to gods and becomes archetypal by silhouetting the human struggle to find meaning within self, society, and the cosmos, a struggle that Santiago enacts in his three-day ordeal. Santiago's voyage, ordeal, and return replicate the traditional pattern of the hero's journey-initiation-return cycle: the hero's journey is community-inspired; his initiation (slaying the dragon, for example) releases reservoirs of vitality needed by his disintegrating community;

and his return restores to his community some wisdom that benefits its renewal.

Other readers find in Santiago's killing of the marlin a child's wish to win the incestuous love of the opposite sex parent and to slay the parent who threatens jealous revenge. Inasmuch as Santiago's actions win the discipleship of Manolin and wrest him away from his father's control, this oedipal reading is not altogether farfetched. Indeed, gigantic ogres are conventionally viewed as substitutes for parental figures. Beckoning from the depths of *Old Man*, then, may be a universally shared, unconscious wish that accounts for the identification many readers have with Santiago.

FICTION

Readers who balk at the moral messages of fables and the symbolic legerdemain of fantasies find that Santiago's three-day ordeal contains the credible events, particularized knowledge, and real-world questions they expect of fictions, especially in one about "the big hunt." For them the novella generates real-world questions about self-measurement:

- Would I have been equal to the task Santiago faced?
- Could I have held up under such an ordeal with my dignity intact?
- Would I have harpooned the marlin when I had triumphed over it?
- Would I have risked going out so far, "beyond all men"?

Even better, Santiago's actions prompt real-world ethical questions:

- Do Santiago's actions arise from a self-validating need to prove himself to others? If so, should ethical value be assigned to that need?
- Can Santiago's actions be viewed as attempts to wrest a youth from his natural parent? If so, are such actions justified?

- Does Santiago jeopardize his ethical integrity by revealing that he cares about other fishermen's approval?
- If Santiago's actions reveal self-glorifying motives, can he still serve as an ethical model?
- Does Santiago truly live by a fraternal ethic that shows love and regard for his various "brothers" if he kills those brothers?

These questions, which I discuss later in this book, indicate the realistic nature of Santiago's actions and ethical dilemmas.

• • •

Despite possible readings of the novella as fable and fantasy, Hemingway's own words dismiss all but a reading as realistic fiction: "I tried to make a real old man, a real boy, a real sea and a real fish and real sharks."[2] This is a forthright declaration of an author's intent, but it can be misleading to read any text according to an author's declared or implied intent. Readers learn to be wary of authors who declare their intentions, if only because as professional storytellers any utterance from their mouths or pens or typewriters or computers may be sheer fabrication. In addition, authors' conscious intentions may be at odds with the unconscious patterns their narratives reveal to readers but conceal from the authors themselves, and so the meanings found in their texts may be quite at odds with what they tried to do. Finally, authors' intentions have limited power over the cultural perspectives, ideological backgrounds, reading strategies, literary experiences, historical predispositions, personal biases, and other factors that contribute to the value—or lack of value—readers find in texts. An author's text controls literally *what* we read, but it has less influence over *how* we read and interpret it.

It is always a reader's task to construct meaning, assign significance, and resolve matters to his or her satisfaction, and different readers—fabulists, fantasists, and fictionalists—construct different meanings and resolve issues differently than others do. It follows that a masterwork is a text that generates a wide array of divergent readings. I think that a mark of the stature of *The Old Man and the Sea* as a masterwork lies in its multiplicity of readings, regardless of whether Ernest Hemingway, a literary critic, or a high school teacher would uniformly agree on those readings as entirely sound or respectable.

3

Critical Reception

The Old Man and the Sea has tumbled from the pedestal on which it initially perched, as has Hemingway's 1940 Spanish Civil War novel, For Whom the Bell Tolls. Hemingway thought the novella "impregnable to criticism," and it is unlikely that his personal estimate of it, given enough time and distance, would have swung from high regard to rejection. Nevertheless, an overview of the book's reputation—in the eyes of Hemingway's friends, reviewers, and literary critics—charts such a swing. That swing surely questions whether Old Man justly belongs in a series of studies of literary masterworks, a question my reader will, I hope, be able to answer after having read this study.

After the dismal review of his 1950 novel Across the River and into the Trees, Hemingway welcomed the praise generated by the typescript he completed by the end of February 1951. He had begun drafting Santiago's story just after the 1950 Christmas holiday but thought of the story as part of a larger novel he was working on, "The Sea Book." He envisioned this bigger novel, which included material that later formed portions of Islands in the Stream, as a segment of an epic, a sea-land-and-air trilogy. The last two segments of that trilogy failed to materialize, but in 1947 Hemingway had drafted the "Bimini" section of his "Sea Book," and in early December 1950 he drafted the "Cuba" section.

On completing the Santiago typescript—26,531 words by his own count—Hemingway began talking of "The Sea Book" as a trilogy, and what we now know as the "Bimini" and "Cuba" sections of *Islands in the Stream* he titled "The Sea When Young" and "The Sea When Absent," respectively. Santiago's story was "The Sea in Being." In early March he launched another story that became the "At Sea" section of *Islands*. By mid-May he realized he had a tetralogy on his hands. Although he assured publisher Charles Scribner that the four-part novel would be ready for publication in 1952, his revisions of the "Bimini" material proceeded slowly.

In the meantime Hemingway showed friends the typescript of Santiago's story. They warmly praised its "mysterious quality," and word of the Santiago story spread, bringing to Cuba a *Cosmopolitan* magazine editor whose enthusiasm resulted in discussions of publishing the complete story in a single issue. Hemingway rejected an offer of $10,000, however, and by October he wrote to Charles Scribner about his pleasure in his story: "This is the prose that I have been working for all my life that should read easily and simply and seem short and yet have all the dimensions of the visible world and the world of a man's spirit. It is as good prose as I can write as of now."[3]

By the following March 1952 Hemingway still had not decided on the story's title. "The Dignity of Man" he felt was pompous, and he disliked "The Sea in Being." About the time he settled on his title, he was under new pressure to let the story be published in a magazine. In May he agreed to have the story published in a single issue of *Life*— for $40,000—and also received confirmation that the novella would be a Book-of-the-Month Club selection, guaranteeing him another $21,000.

The *Life* and the Book-of-the-Month Club sales were not disappointing. In two days *Life* sold 5,300,000 copies of its 1 September issue, and the first printing of the Book-of-the-Month Club edition sold

153,000 copies. Scribners' trade edition of the book catapulted to the tops of the best-seller lists and sat there for half a year.

Early book reviews of *Old Man* were favorable, and the title of Edward Weeks's *Atlantic* review summed up many readers' opinions: "Hemingway at His Best." In the *Nation* Harvey Breit rhapsodized about it as "a great and 'true' novel, touching and terrible, tragic and happy," remarking especially on Hemingway's ability to transpose "the mystique of fishing" into "a universal condition of life." In the *New York Times Book Review* Robert Gorham Davis extolled the novella as "a tale superbly told" and marveled at its ability to imply "a human continuity that far transcends an individual relationship." Fanny Butcher in the *Chicago Sunday Tribune* claimed the book to be an epic and "a great American classic of man's battle with a titan of the sea," and Joseph Henry Jackson in the *San Francisco Chronicle* called it "as perfect a piece of work as Hemingway has ever done," a "miracle-play of Man against Fate." Henry Seidel Canby, in *Book-of-the-Month Club News*, chimed in with, "the best fishing story in English" and complimented Hemingway's artistry: "Through Hemingway's matchless skill, a fishing story becomes a masterpiece." Even William Faulkner, in *Shenandoah*, found the book to be "his best" and conceded, "Time may show it to be the best single piece of any of us, I mean his and my contemporaries."[4]

Other reviewers' praise, however, was qualified. Orville Prescott in the *New York Times* objected that Santiago was more a symbolic attitude toward life than a man, a character whose poetically rendered thoughts border on artificiality. In the *Hudson Review* R. W. B. Lewis complained that Hemingway "verges on the antic" when he "tampers" with Santiago, as when he "makes him dream of lions on the beach." Mark Schorer's review in *New Republic*, while commending the novella's fable-like virtues, also faulted an occasional "murky" paragraph "where the writing wavers, its pure lucidity is muddied by all that hulking personality which, at his worst, Hemingway has made all too familiar." *Partisan Review*'s Delmore Schwartz tolerated the novella as a "virtuoso performance" and applauded the "pure vividness of presentation" during the fishing narrative, but he disliked Heming-way's handling of Santiago's emotions, criticizing it for having "a margin of self-consciousness and a mannerism of assertion."[5]

A handful of out-and-out detractors called *Old Man* "the poor man's *Moby Dick*." In *Commonweal* Seymour Krim dismissed the novella on the grounds that Hemingway was repeating and embellishing themes and ideas from his earlier work, showing no new vision or fresh sensibility. In *Commentary* Philip Rahv refused the label of "masterpiece" that other reviewers assigned the book, predicted that it would not "be placed among Hemingway's major writings," and complained that its expression of emotion, though genuine, was "so elemental in its totality as to exact nothing from us beyond instant assent." John W. Aldridge, in *Virginia Quarterly Review*, called the novella "a work of distinctly minor Hemingway fiction," finding its style "oddly colorless and flat" and its thematic concerns with "the strong man struggling to survive amid the hostile pressures of a purely physical world" a poor substitute for the theme that had best served Hemingway—"the shell-shocked, traumatic man struggling to preserve himself . . . from psychic destruction." In *Masses and Mainstream* Milton Howard's Marxist review criticized the novella because of Santiago's isolation from meaningful social struggle.[6]

Despite its detractors, *Old Man* won the 1953 Pulitzer Prize and the American Academy of Arts and Letters' Award of Merit Medal for the Novel and contributed to Hemingway's selection for the 1954 Nobel Prize for Literature. In addition, Hollywood filmed it as a major 1958 attraction starring Spencer Tracy, who with Leland Hayward bought the film rights—and Hemingway's services as technical adviser—for $150,000.

In 1967 the novella sold 275,000 paperback copies and earned $100,000 in foreign royalties as a school text in French, German, Italian, and Japanese. Among literary critics and scholars its reputation was eroding, however, and in the 1980s fewer than two dozen articles, notes, or chapters were published about *Old Man*, as contrasted, for example, to more than 80 items on *The Sun Also Rises*.

Such was not the case in the 15 years after the novella's publication. Between 1952 and 1967 scholars were respectful of, if not downright reverential toward, the book. Humanistic biases influenced much of this predominantly religious and mythological criticism, which characteristically examined the novella's emphasis on mankind's nobler traits and moral heroics and admired Santiago's valiant struggle against nature and its forces, plucking as he does a victory for humanity from the jaws of defeat.

Representative critics with humanistic approaches are Philip Young, Leo Gurko, and Clinton S. Burhans. Calling the novella "an epic metaphor, a contest where even the problem of moral right and wrong seems paltry if not irrelevant," Young esteemed the story's "veneration for humanity, for what can be done and endured, and this grasp of man's kinship with the other creatures of the world, and with the world itself, is itself a victory of substantial proportions. It is the knowledge that a simple man is capable of such decency, dignity and even heroism, and that his struggle can be seen in heroic terms, that largely distinguishes this book." Likewise, Gurko found that Hemingway continued in the romantic tradition and created "a hero whose triumph consists of stretching his own powers to their absolute limits regardless of the physical results." Burhans celebrated the fraternal interdependency represented in Santiago, "a noble and tragic individualism revealing what man can do in an indifferent universe which defeats him, and the love he can feel for such a universe and his humility before it."[7]

Another trio of critics read the novella through a strongly religious filter. Carlos Baker concurred with humanistic critics in finding Hemingway's "ancient mariner" compassionate, courageous, and fraternal, but he emphasized the work's Christian symbolism, Santiago's piety and suffering, and his experience as a form of martyrdom that made the novella a biblical parable. A year later, Joseph Waldmeir interpreted the novella's religious symbols and numerology as part of an allegorical commentary of secularized religion. Arvin S. Wells, acknowledging the text's Christian analogies and Santiago's saintly humility, faith, and charity, concluded that the old fisherman's capacity for suffering transformed his ordeal into a religious mystery and that his identification with the marlin's "beauty, nobility, courage, calmness and endurance" redeemed his own "life from meaninglessness and futility."[8]

A pair of mythic readers, Earl Rovit and Bickford Sylvester, also praised the novella. Rovit found a Jungian quest-initiation-return ritual in Santiago's journey and in "his final rites of purification far out in the wilderness, beyond the glow of lights from Havana." Characteristic of all archetypal heroes, who act out the human struggle with self, society, and universal ideals, Santiago returns to his community, bringing "back from his isolation a fragmented gift offering to his fellows, an imperfect symbol to suggest where he has been and what he found there" so that his "experience will be filtered down to the others [of his community] who are less sensitive or less prone to enflesh the mysteries" of a transcendent event. Unlike conventional humanistic readings of the novella, Sylvester found little human interdependence or harmony between man and nature. For him the novella set forth a principle of "universal order"—the independence of all men, whose "opposition to nature is paradoxically revealed as necessary to vitality in the natural field upon which the action takes place." Santiago's "compassionate violence" against the marlin shows that the "coincidence between the journey of the sun and the various rounds of combat implies consonance with an order which is supra-animate—which is universal in the observable physical world." Calling the novella's myth "profoundly humanistic," Sylvester also found it "a modern parable of man's fallen state in which the universe requires man to overcome more in order to achieve what is necessary for all creatures."[9]

With the notable exception of Wirt Williams's chapter on the novella in 1981, which regards it as the culmination of Hemingway's complex tragic vision, *The Old Man and the Sea* has come under continued attack from realistic critics since the mid-1960s. Two attacks came early in the decade. In a 1961 *Encounter* book review Philip Toynbee wrote "that the book is meretricious from beginning to end, that the archaic false simplicities of its style are insufferable, that the sentimentality is flagrant and outrageous and that the myth is tediously enforced." A year later Robert P. Weeks found the book "pieced out with an extraordinary quantity of fakery," citing the notions that Santiago had cat's eyes and could once "see quite well in the dark"; that Santiago could detect the marlin's gender and know of its nibbling on the bait at the end of his pencil-thick, 600-foot-long line; and that Santiago knows better than a meteorologist the signs of a coming hurricane. Weeks also cited factual errors: the alleged eight rows of teeth in the mako shark; the Portuguese man-of-war's presence near his skiff, "fully six months before an animal this size would normally appear in Cuban waters"; and Santiago's incorrect identification of Rigel as the night's first star ("Rigel does not appear in Cuban skies at sunset in September, but some five hours after Santiago sees it"). By 1966 Philip Young had withdrawn his praise for the novella. He objected to its "affectation of simplicity," its autobiographical self-admiration, and its unrealistic detail of young Manolin carrying to Santiago's boat the harpoon, the gaff, and three-fourths of a mile of pencil-thick fishing line, no light burden, to be sure.[10]

Three other realistic critics joined the attack. In 1967 German critic Wolfgang Wittkowski dismantled the novella's Christian symbolism and argued that Santiago exhibits a boxer's ethic, wishes to perform his heroic contest before a spectator, values his self-esteem as a fighter and a crucifier and a killer, and takes pleasure in "confrontation and victory in competitive sport." Responding to the mythic readings of *Old Man* Claire Rosenfield acknowledged the folktale and mythic resonances in the novella's motif of a tribal hero's confrontation with a totem animal—an oversized native creature whom the hero fears, admires, and eats of. She also argued, however, that the references to baseball "tend to fuse and confuse a way of life with a mode of entertainment," that Hemingway's old fisherman has a "banal range" of perceptions, and that Hemingway's "emphatically male bias makes the purposive mingling of game and rite ridiculous" because baseball lacks all "suggestion of cult participation or identification." The novella got its most sustained denunciation from Jackson J. Benson in

1969. While respecting Hemingway's "careful and deliberate execution" of his artistry in the novella, Benson concluded that "Santiago becomes a figure too removed, almost precious in his highly stylized role, and his tragedy, with every carefully contrived suggestive detail in its proper orbit, lacks the spontaneity of moving passion." Claiming that "the fish is a violation of the poetic terms of the allegory" and that "art is brought to the edge of the ridiculous by its very artfulness," Benson wrote, "The story does not use ritual; it is a ritual—almost a text for 'worship.' "[11]

In the 1970s occasional articles and chapters on *Old Man* appeared, but they tended to be minor essays: a textual critic linked the novella's foot motif to the constellation Orion's left-foot star, Rigel (Kenneth G. Johnston); scholars uncovered more of the novella's biblical and baseball allusions (Joseph H. Flora and George Monteiro); an esthetician attempted to resurrect it by attending to its generic identity as a lyric novel of organic unity (Linda Wagner); and a New Critical ironist probed the baseball allusions to argue that their symbolic "allurements" tempt "the old man from his true calling" and prove the superiority of his achievements over Joe DiMaggio's (Sam S. Baskett).[12]

Revisionist critics, who examine a text's complexities without the burden of humanistic interpretation, date from Ben Stoltzfus's all-but-neglected chapter on "Hemingway's Battle with God," an insightful and occasionally ingenious 1978 rereading of the Christian motifs and allusions in the novella. He variously identifies it as "a pagan poem to existential man," as a text whose "christological imagery . . . is essentially non-Christian," as a covert story of Santiago's proud "challenge to Creation" and Hemingway's slaying of Christian values, and as a celebration "of pride rather than humility—an exaltation of man with only perfunctory obeisance to God." In 1983 I brought ignored biographical, psychological, and ethical questions to the novella. I accused Santiago of self-serving motives, found psychoanalytic depths that universalize the tale's oedipal dimensions, and explored problems between Hemingway and his three sons.[13]

Finally, the novella has not been immune to contemporary critical theory. In 1984 it received its only feminist reading, Martin Swan finding misogyny well entrenched in the novella's treatment of its four female "characters"—the female tourist, Santiago's wife, the sea, and the Portuguese man-of-war. Ben Stoltzfus's Lacanian reading presents yet another direction: his semiotic strategies reveal the unconscious links between Santiago's pride, his dreams of lions, and his daydreams of Joe DiMaggio.[14]

• • •

An account of the critical reception would be incomplete without three more citations—one personal and two biographical. The personal one is confessional. In the early 1970s I found it nearly impossible to read or teach *The Old Man and the Sea*, which to me appeared totally at odds with Hemingway's statement, "I tried to make a real old man, a real boy, a real sea and a real fish and real sharks." Santiago seemed to be a mythically abstract entity at worst, a patron saint for Boy Scouts at best. He had little in common with recognizable human beings, whose idiosyncracies and crotchets, egoistic elements, and repressed memory traces of embarrassing episodes from the past help make them real. In the mid-1970s I explored anew Santiago's motives, however, and discovered quite a believable fellow mortal.

One biographical citation is to Hemingway's third son's estimate of *Old Man*. During the decade-long period when father and son were not on speaking terms, Gregory irreverently called the novel "as sickly a bucket of sentimental slop as was ever scrubbed off the bar-room floor." The other biographical citation is from Kenneth Lynn, whose 1987 biography, elbowing its way to the forefront of several contemporary biographies of Hemingway, representatively sums up the "accepted" attitude toward the novella:

> Today, there is only one question worth asking about *The Old Man*. How could a book that lapses repeatedly into lachrymose sentimentality and is relentlessly pseudo-Biblical, that mixes cute

talk about baseball ("I fear both the Tigers of Detroit and the Indians of Cleveland") with crucifixion symbolism of the most appalling crudity ("he slept face down on the newspapers with his arms out straight and the palms of his hands up"), have evoked such a storm of applause from highbrows and middlebrows alike—and in such overwhelming numbers?[15]

Lynn's and Gregory Hemingway's negative perceptions throw down the gauntlet for any challenger. The following reading picks up that challenge.

A READING

Ernest Hemingway in Bimini, 1935. *Photograph courtesy of the Ernest Hemingway Foundation and the John Fitzgerald Kennedy Library Hemingway Collection*

Ernest Hemingway in Peru, 1956.
Photograph courtesy of the Ernest Hemingway Foundation and the John Fitzgerald Kennedy Library Hemingway Collection

4

A Preliminary Reading

A masterwork speaks across historical periods to a broad range of readers; it also deals freshly or complexly with recurrent human issues, engaging readers emotionally and intellectually as they measure its treatment of those issues against the yardsticks of daily existence. A brief look at the sources that Hemingway drew from highlights the idealized character of Santiago, but a skeptical examination of some of the aspects of that idealized character can begin to show the novella satisfying these criteria of a masterwork.

SANTIAGO'S UNIDEALIZED PROTOTYPES

In an *Esquire* "letter" dated April 1936—"On the Blue Water: A Gulf Stream Letter"—Hemingway tells the anecdote on which 15 years later he based his novella:

> Another time an old man fishing alone in a skiff out of Cabanas hooked a great marlin that, on the heavy sashcord handline, pulled

the skiff far out to sea. Two days later the old man was picked up by fishermen sixty miles to the eastward, the head and forward part of the marlin lashed alongside. What was left of the fish, less than half, weighed eight hundred pounds. The old man had stayed with him a day, a night, a day and another night while the fish swam deep and pulled the boat. When he had come up the old man had pulled the boat up on him and harpooned him. Lashed alongside the sharks had hit him and the old man had fought them out alone in the Gulf Stream in a skiff, clubbing them, stabbing at them, lunging at them with an oar until he was exhausted and the sharks had eaten all that they could hold. He was crying in the boat when the fishermen picked him up, half crazy from his loss, and the sharks were circling the boat.[16]

The old fisherman of this anecdote, allegedly based on Carlos Guiterrez, the first skipper of Hemingway's fishing boat *Pilar*, is not Santiago: he lacks Santiago's self-sufficiency (he cannot return his skiff to harbor and requires rescue), endurance (he sits or lies exhausted in his boat after only a two-day ordeal when fishermen find him), and philosophic resignation (his crying indicates that he feels the futility of his efforts, the folly of his expectations, the disappointment of his financial loss, or the rapacity of the sharks that have feasted on his fish).

The anecdote also implies that the old fisherman is either unskilled, inconsiderate, or desperate when he kills his marlin, for he "had pulled the boat up on him and harpooned him." The old fisherman seems to have rushed his killing, eager to sink his harpoon into the fish before it escapes. A harpooning in the dorsal side of the marlin would stand small chance of a quick, clean kill because the harpoon would have to penetrate bone and muscle before reaching a vital organ. This fisherman's dorsal harpooning, then, risks inflicting pain on the marlin before it expires. In contrast, Santiago spends considerable time and energy, even risking loss of consciousness, in turning over the marlin before harpooning it. Seven times he turns the marlin over only to have it right itself and swim off. Not until the eighth try does Santiago succeed and harpoon it through the ventral side for a quick dispatch, the marlin coming alive "with his death in him" (94) for one leap out of the water before crashing back into it, dead.

Further, the anecdote tells that its fisherman fights the sharks, "clubbing them, stabbing at them, lunging at them with an oar." Like Santiago, he has lost implements with which to defend his marlin's carcass and is forced to resort to such ineffective weapons as his oars. Because the anecdote gives no sense of the fisherman's motive for defending his marlin, a reader can attribute to him exclusively commercial motives: when rescued he is crying and "half crazy with his loss," suggesting concern about the loss of money the fish would have brought him. In Hemingway's novella, however, Santiago's defense of his marlin seems motivated by love and respect for its noble beauty, which he loathes to see desecrated, and by fraternal regard for this noble brother, whose mutilation seems to prove Santiago's treachery to his brothers. The anecdotal fisherman is no shore-hugger, fearful of the contest with a giant marlin, but he is no Santiago, either.

Neither is another prototype, whom Gregorio Fuentes, the *Pilar's* second skipper, remembers.[17] Near the end of the 1940s he and Hemingway witnessed a man and a boy in a rickety old boat being swiftly dragged by a fish the man had hooked. Throttled at full speed, the *Pilar* could scarcely keep up with the boat when Hemingway approached to offer help. The thin, strong, shirtless man screamed at them, "Get out of here, you sons of bitches! Leave me alone!" Hemingway and Gregorio backed off and watched the battle for half a day. Hemingway finally sent Gregorio with some provisions in an auxiliary boat. As he approached, again the man shouted obscenities and told him to "Get away," which Gregorio did but not before he drew near enough to throw the package of provisions into the old boat. The outcome of the episode goes unrecorded, but clearly Santiago bears no resemblance to this fisherman.

SANTIAGO'S IDEALIZED CHARACTER

Most new readers of Hemingway's novella find Santiago unquestionably an admirable character. When measured against various yardsticks—heroic, saintly, and parental—he fares so well that he seems impervious to criticism.

Santiago as Hero
As a heroic character he struggles against the natural forces of the sea, the marlin, and the sharks as well as against his own physical limitations. His resoluteness to persevere and conquer the marlin reveals the heroic fiber expected of exemplars who model courageous behavior in the face of danger and risk. In harpooning the great fish he risks being crushed by the pained fish in its death throes, and his hand-to-hand, three-day combat, without benefit of modern technology, evokes images of great warriors pushed to the limits of their capacities. Indeed, Santiago's careful consideration of logistics— of just how to play the fish in order to subdue it—makes it easy to regard his maneuvers as ones of military prowess: his battlefield is the Gulf Stream. By going out too far, he distinguishes himself as a man who leaves behind conventional routines and braves the dangerous unknown, risking life in the adventure. The marlin's choice, Santiago tells himself, "had been to stay in the deep dark water far out beyond all snares and traps and treacheries. My choice was to go there to find him beyond all people. Beyond all people in the world" (50). In doing so he becomes a "hero with a thousand faces," the archetypal hero described by Joseph Campbell who follows the journey-initiation-return cycle. Santiago's actions invite readers to say about him what Joseph Conrad's Marlow says of Lord Jim—that he's "an individual in the forefront of his kind, whose acts and the obscure truth involved in them were momentous enough to affect mankind's conception of itself."[18]

Although Santiago's victory over the marlin may ensure his status as hero, he also frees a hostage. In heroic romances the hostage is an imprisoned maiden whose freedom results from the hero's vanquishing of some dark agent of evil. Here Santiago's victory releases Manolin from bondage to his father's tyranny and insistence that Manolin abandon his long-time tutor and friend to fish with a man who has little regard for the boy. The friendship between Manolin and Santiago at the novella's end mirrors the erotic bonding that customarily rewards a hero's deeds.

Santiago as Saint Readers who find the hero's crown tilting uneasily on Santiago's brow may wish to replace it with the saint's halo. Santiago exudes a strong religious sensibility. This "Saint James," as his name translates, conjures up Saint Francis of Assisi, known for his love for the birds of the air and creatures of the land. Although Santiago maligns the iridescent, gelatinous Portuguese man-of-war as "You whore" (35) and the shovel-nosed sharks as "hateful, bad-smelling scavengers" (108), Santiago loves the creatures of his world—green, hawk-bill, loggerhead, and trunkback turtles, porpoises, the warbler resting on his fishing line, the wild ducks passing overhead, fighting cocks, dolphins, flying fish, lions, the eel-like gray sucking fish that swim around the marlin, Gulf weed shrimp, and even the Mako shark.

Santiago's saintliness is also revealed in his response to the marlin's three unexpected lurches. During the first night it makes a lurch "that pulled [Santiago] down on his face and made a cut below his eye" (52). The marlin's second lurch, as if cued by Santiago's calling it "a friend," nearly pulls him overboard and cuts the flesh of his hand (55–56). The marlin's third lurch comes on the second night while Santiago naps (82). The rushing line jerks his fist into his face, burns his body and right hand, cuts his left hand, and, as the marlin jumps several times, pulls Santiago's face into the fillet of dolphin he had cut earlier. Not once does Santiago respond to these hurts and indignities with so much as a curse or a hint of irritation in his voice for the fish. This absence of antagonism and resentment toward his adversary suggests a saintlike and immediate forgiveness.

Santiago's fraternal ethic makes the best argument for his saintliness. He overtly regards the marlin, porpoises, flying fish and the stars as his brothers and indirectly includes the lions of his dreams, Joe DiMaggio, the "negro of Cienfuegos," and the man-of-war bird in his fraternity. Santiago also treats the boy Manolin as an equal, in contrast to the fisherman to whom Manolin's parents send him after Santiago's

40 fishless days. That man treats Manolin as an "inferior," never letting him share the duties of being a fisherman. When Santiago tells himself, "There are three things that are my brothers, the fish and my two hands" (64), he also equates Manolin as his brother, for the boy's name literally means "small hand" and figuratively means "little brother." The attitude of brotherhood that Santiago exemplifies is an embodiment of a brother's keeper whose every act exhibits the altruistic behavior expected of a saint.

Santiago as Parent This Hemingway hero behaves with the compassion and nurturance commonly associated with a parental—even maternal—figure. Throughout his combat with the marlin, for instance, he compassionately grieves that it must go without food and wishes he could feed it. Likewise he remorsefully recalls catching a female marlin whose mate stayed throughout her fight and seemed to suffer when separated from her. Calling the episode "the saddest thing I ever saw with them," Santiago acknowledges that he and Manolin "begged her pardon and butchered her promptly" (50). He feels sorrow for turtles, which often are the sport of people who butcher them to watch their hearts beat hours after dismemberment. He is also sorry for seabirds, "especially the small, delicate dark terns that were always flying and looking and almost never finding" (29). It is not surprising that Santiago asks forgiveness of the marlin and is sorrowful that their combat has ended in the marlin's mutilation by the marauding sharks.

Santiago's compassionate sensitivity to and desire to alleviate others' distress is matched by his nurturance. His contest with the marlin may initially seem to portray a stereotypically male will to dominate, but his victory is a means to an end rather than an end in itself. Central to Santiago's motivation is his need to regain the community's respect so that Manolin can return to him for proper tutelage, thus making the fishing story a family drama. Since he was five years old Manolin has been nurtured by Santiago, a mother figure, but when Santiago's luck turns bad, the boy's biological father removes him from Santiago's instruction and sends him to fish with a man who treats him as an inferior, threatening to undo Santiago's teaching and abort any further nurturing Santiago can give the boy. Santiago's perseverance in his ordeal resembles that of the single parent who suffers hardships and triumphs over adversity to provide what he or she believes is best for a child. Santiago's repeated wish that Manolin were with him during the ordeal translates as a wish not for a helper, a little hand, but for an instructional opportunity for the boy to learn how to battle a fearsome adversary singlehandedly. In fact, Manolin pledges his discipleship to Santiago at novella's end, declaring, "We will fish together now for I still have to learn" (125).

The gentleness that Santiago shows Manolin, both before and after the ordeal, further argues his parental character, as does Santiago's tolerance for the natural rights of the sharks to feed on his marlin. Hateful though they are to him, he never resorts to acrimony toward them.

• • •

These readings of Santiago's character as heroic, saintly, and parental liquify into an idealized, androgynous figure—a parent that is of indeterminate gender. Santiago embodies a host of virtues, including selflessness, courage, considerateness, wisdom, reliability, industriousness, perseverance, loyalty, and trustworthiness. In addition, his esthetic sensibility allows him to appreciate the lavender-striped beauty of the marlin, the blue and gold albacore, the purple-spotted, burnished-gold dolphin, and the blue and silver Mako shark. Finally, a nondogmatic religious sensibility allows Santiago to invoke Catholic prayers but without belief in their efficacy other than as commonplace rituals that he will neither exploit blasphemously nor defer to piously. Santiago is an exemplary model for every parent who desires both professional acknowledgments and uncelebrated domestic humaneness.

Santiago's Skeptical Reader

Old Man seduces many readers into admiring Santiago as an idealized figure—hero, saint, brother, mother, or father. Such admiration leads some readers into inflated interpretations of the text that remove it from the realm of daily issues and enshrine it in a mystical temple of sacred literature. It can disarm readers of the skepticism that educated readers bring to every text, literary or not, and to any claim to authority or truth. Skepticism is the reader's best defense against being duped by a text or an author into taking that text at face value. As Robert Scholes convincingly argues in *Semiotics and Interpretation*, the common ingredient of all literary texts is duplicity.[19] Readers need to doubt the value and validity of their own and others' interpretations of a work, especially if those interpretations ignore the probing questions that the skeptical reader insists on. A skeptical look at Santiago's fraternal ethic and the novella's religious imagery should deidealize *Old Man* and show how its complex issues can intellectually engage readers.

Santiago's Fraternal Ethic Saturated with motifs of brotherhood and fraternal love, the novella invites readings that find Santiago to be an exemplary brother's keeper, a model of altruism. Certainly his regard for Manolin and the marlin is evidence of his fraternal ethic, for Santiago's attitudes toward the pair are benevolent and respectful. Nevertheless, a skeptical reader questions that recurring motif, whose frequency suggests the presence of a compulsion in Santiago to function fraternally, just as any excessive behavior suggests an obsessive need to display only that behavior and thereby to hide or deny the existence of its opposite. This is the usual form that reaction formation takes, say psychologists, in the behavior of both neurotics and normal people. The text offers ample evidence that Santiago's fraternal ethic is a facade for altruism's opposite, egoism.

One clue to Santiago's self-centered or egoistic ethic is his repeated wish that Manolin were in the skiff to help bring in the marlin. His motive for that wish can be the sublimated, nurturing interest in Manolin's continued education, as I have argued, but the motive also can be raw self-interest—a wish for Manolin's help, for a witness to his own heroic endurance, or for an ally to share blame should the ordeal somehow fail. The repeated wish also indicates that the old man resents Manolin for failing to be with him in the skiff—for obeying his father and abandoning Santiago 45 days earlier. Proof of this resentment comes on Santiago's first night with the marlin. After wishing that the boy was with him, he thinks, "No one should be alone in their old age" (48). The repeated wish, then, masks Santiago's anger at Manolin for failing to pledge discipleship to the superior fisherman-tutor—himself.

A more significant proof of the hollowness of Santiago's fraternal ethic is his killing of the marlin and the other fish he calls "brothers." His profession of fisherman requires the death of his prey, but he continually mouths benevolent feelings for his prey, expresses concern for the marlin's pain, empathizes with its foodless flight, and apologizes to it for having gone out too far. Santiago displays an anthropomorphic identification with the creatures he hunts and likens them to humans, but hypocrites reveal themselves by the discrepancy between their words and deeds. Because Santiago kills the creatures his words call "brother," his acts show him to be a fratricide—his brothers' killer, not their keeper. The egoism of his ethic, then, leads him to pursue mutually exclusive goals—to be a successful fisherman whose killing wins professional respect and to be a benevolent brother whose love for all living creatures wins humanitarian regard. If the zealot who murders his fellow nationalists in the name of patriotism cannot escape ethical censure and criminal punishment, then we apply a curious double standard to Santiago if we accept both his killing and his fraternal feelings without noting ethical paradox.

Santiago's fraternal ethic is self-serving in that it also frees him from domestic obligations. The legitimacy of the duties owed to parents, spouses, or children compel one to perform those duties or reckon with the guilt, betrayal, accusations, and other consequences of not doing so. A brother's claims, however, are not easily enforced: Santiago can feel good about his Samaritanism and win others' regard or ignore others' plight with only minor guilt, excusing himself with the notion that the duty belonged to someone else. Santiago takes pleasure in his fraternal feelings toward terns, warblers, turtles, and the marlin, but those feelings require no corresponding actions from him on their behalf.

Finally, Santiago's status as widower also tends to discredit the old fisherman's fraternal ethic. The narrative mentions that Santiago has turned the photograph of his wife against the wall but never mentions her again, and although Santiago dreams and daydreams, he never thinks of her. Indeed, neither the text nor Santiago's dreams mentions any children begotten from that marriage or any brothers, sisters, mother, or father. Santiago, then, is without family. His only relationship that approximates a familial one is with Manolin, and the loss of Manolin's companionship 45 days before the novella's events begin raises questions of whether Santiago perseveres in his three-day ordeal to wrest Manolin away from his father and win himself a "son" he can treat as a brother. If this motive prompts Santiago's ordeal, then his so-called fraternal ethic is strongly tainted with parental possessiveness.

These skeptical views of Santiago's fraternal ethic ensure the novella's status as a masterwork, for they widen the range of interpretation Santiago elicits and show that the text deals complexly with the recurrent issues of altruism and egotism.

Religious Imagery and Allusions Santiago's fraternal ethic has its roots in the New Testament's parable of the Good Samaritan and in Genesis's account of Cain's murdering his brother, Abel, which results in Cain's rejoinder to God's censure, "Am I my brother's keeper?," and Santiago's physical torment is often compared to Jesus' sufferings on the cross. A skeptical reader examines the novella's religious imagery and allusions and asks whether they contribute to the text's stature as a masterwork.

Santiago is often regarded a Christ figure, and his love for all living creatures and forebearance in physical pain are attributes that support this reading. His brief conversation with the warbler that sits on the taut line just before the marlin's first lurch echoes Jesus' admonition to his followers when they try to keep children away from him: "Suffer the little children to come unto me." Santiago's badly injured hands also evoke the hands of the crucified Christ, and three overt allusions to crucifixion reinforce this image. First, Santiago sees the pair of shovel-nosed sharks swimming toward the captured marlin, already a mutilated victim of the Mako shark: " 'Ay,' he said aloud. There is no translation for this word and perhaps it is just a noise such a man might make, involuntarily, feeling the nail go through his hand and into the wood" (107). Then, once back on shore, Santiago shoulders his furled mast and climbs to the hill toward his shack, falling several times, a blatant reference to Christ's struggle to carry the cross up the hill Cavalry. Finally, Santiago lets his weary body fall onto his bed with "his arms out straight and the palms of his hands up" (122).

A skeptical reader finds problems in all of these religious allusions and analogues. Santiago shares too few traits in common with Christ: Christ is a fisher of men, but Santiago is merely a fisherman; Christ is a figure with a divine mission, Santiago one with a secular mission (to bring back an oversized fish); Christ is a martyr who willingly but reluctantly dies for his convictions, Santiago is a persevering champion who is willing to die only to win a battle with a fish; Christ is a teacher of spiritual and ethical wisdom, Santiago is a professional with skill and slogans to impart. A skeptical reader, in short, balks at the comparison, however well intentioned: correspondences between two characters must be deeper than a few generalized traits and strained analogues. Indeed, many with knowledge and respect for the New Testament's accounts of the Christ story are affronted by the facile linking of Santiago's name with Christ's.

Nevertheless, the religious allusions enrich the novella and contribute to its stature as a masterwork. Although those allusions do not withstand close viewing, they allow readers to consider whether they should find in Santiago a Christ. The ability to suggest meaning and significance that ripples beyond the text is one of the traits that we expect to find in a masterwork—power to provoke thought and conflicting interpretation rather than to establish a firm allegorical connection between two texts. In other words, a skeptical reader does not automatically reject an interpretation but instead tests readings to determine the merit of the evidence and explanation brought forth to support a reading. A skeptical reader remains alert to many possible readings.

5

Structure

The structure of *The Old Man and the Sea*—a chronological account of events, the most basic form of storytelling—makes few of the demands on readers that intricate fictions do. It begins late on the eighty-fourth day that Santiago has not caught a fish, with Manolin helping him home with his gear, and ends four days later with Manolin talking and seeing to the needs of the exhausted old man. Hemingway wrote one novel that covers a shorter span of time—Robert Jordan's three-day bridge-blowing mission in the Spanish Civil War novel, *For Whom the Bell Tolls*—but complicated that novel with a dense backgrounding of three of the four structural devices that rhetorically heighten a fiction's effects—flashbacks, subplots, and stories-within-the story. (It lacks only the fourth structural device, a frame.) When compared to that epic novel, *Old Man* seems structurally quite simple, but its frame and flashback memories widen the context and significance of the novella's basic fishing tale. Those two structural devices, however, are secondary to the fishing tale itself—the central structural block of the novella—which warrants initial attention.

THE ARCHETYPAL FISHING STORY

As a story about man's battle with the forces of nature, the account of Santiago's three-day ordeal is artistically satisfying. It is suspenseful. It

39

entices readers to discover whether Santiago will lose the hooked giant marlin, whether the pair will make it back to port intact and whether Santiago will subdue the sharks and survive his ordeal. The novella sustains tension with a series of conflicts—Santiago's will and intelligence pitted against the marlin's instincts and power, Santiago's protection of the dead marlin against the sharks' devouring of its carcass, his physical deteriorations against his mental resourcefulness, his hunter's skill in killing against his humane inclinations, his remorseful moralizing against his self-congratulatory pride. Finally, the novella satisfyingly renders an archetypal event by localizing an incident and simultaneously making it both particular and universal. An old man who puts to sea in a boat to catch a fish is the stuff of innumerable anecdotes and tales told by waterfront peoples the world over. To tell that story so that those peoples can identify themselves and their culture in it—and landlocked urban and rural people also can identify with and find meaning in Santiago's big hunt—shows storytelling ability.

Part of Hemingway's storytelling ability lies in Santiago's ironic self-importance. He is proud of going out too far, beyond all men, and asks to be singled out among all men, but he has gone out beyond only the men he knows of. Other men and women in other seaside communities have risked their lives by "going too far out," and still larger numbers of men and women in other occupations have metaphorically gone out beyond others as explorers, scientists, saints, entrepreneurs, or athletes.

The special storytelling feature that universalizes Santiago's experiences is the structural quantification with which Hemingway renders them. He maintains a steady tattoo of numbers throughout the fishing portion of the novella, as the following list indicates:

Q: How many baits does Santiago set out?
A: Four.

Q: How many green-sapped sticks does he loop his lines onto for bobbers?
A: Three.

Q: At what depth are his baits?
A: Forty, 75, 100, and 175 fathoms.

Q: How many fresh tuna had Manolin brought to him?
A: Two.

Q: At two hours after sunrise on the eighty-fifth day, how many boats can Santiago see?
A: Three.

Q: How many times does the circling man-of-war bird unsuccessfully dive after the flying fish chased by dolphin?
A: Six.

Q: How many kinds of turtles does Santiago feel sorry for?
A: Four.

Q: How often does he drink a cup of shark-liver oil?
A: Every day.

Q: How many times does the marlin gently pull on the bait before it fully bites and takes off with it?
A: Six.

Q: How many 40-fathom coils of line in reserve does Santiago make fast to his line before he sets the hook in the marlin?
A: Three.

Q: After he sets the hook, for how many hours does the marlin swim steadily out to sea before Santiago takes a drink from his water bottle?
A: Four.

Q: How many times does Santiago urinate over the side of the boat?
A: Once.

Q: How many dolphins swim around the boat on the first night?
A: Two.

Q. How many times does he wish for something?
A: Nineteen.

Q: How many times does he wish the boy were with him?
A: Five.

Q: How many times does the marlin lurch, hurting Santiago?
A: Three.

Q: In his lifetime how many marlin of over 1,000 pounds has Santiago caught?
A: Two.

Q. How many Our Fathers and Hail Marys will he say if he catches the marlin?
A: On the second day he promises 10, but when he's pulling in the circling marlin on the third day, 100.

Q: How many times does Santiago feel himself on the brink of fainting when he's pulling in the marlin for the kill?
A: Eight.

Q: How many times does he sit down with the mast before he reaches his shack?
A: Five.

One interpretation of this use of numbers is that it is a bookkeeper's or cashier's approach to experience—someone who assumes that life's experiences yield meaning when quantified. This is, after all, a chronologically sequenced tale that counts off sunrises and sunsets as the story progresses. Another interpretation views the number patterns as an individual representation of a universal theme—human beings battling with nature. The itemized particulars of Santiago's experience are unique, but this numerical abstracting shifts them to the level of a representative experience, one replicated by numerous men and women and therefore capable of being magnified to mythic and archetypal dimensions.

Structure

The number of triplets and sevens in the novella suggests religious patternings and a transcendent significance invoking patterns of cyclical experiences. In addition, the novella records cycles of the sunrise and sunset, day and night, seasons of the year, and victory and defeat. These cycles bring to mind the story's repeated image of the circle: the man-of-war bird leads Santiago to the marlin by circling over the flying fish chased by the school of dolphin; the marlin circles the boat again and again while Santiago brings it to his harpoon; Santiago makes a wide geographic loop with the fish, being pulled by it northwest, then north, then east, and then towing it, lashed to his skiff, southwest to port. These circles, as well as the repetition of numbers, establish a harmony of recurring cycles that give the story its unity and archetypal reverberations. Two more circles in the novella—its frame and flashbacks—are more rigorous in their assessment of Santiago than the archetypal structure is, as is often the case when an abstract concept confronts the particulars of an individual case.

THE CHARACTER-COMPLICATING FRAME

A frame is a narrative event that surrounds a story somewhat as a picture frame encloses a painting. In the New Testament the parable of the Good Samaritan is framed at the beginning by the episode of a lawyer who questions Jesus, asking what he must do to inherit eternal life. That frame adds a second level of meaning to the parable: without the frame it is a didactic tale about how the lawyer must be his brother's keeper to inherit eternal life; the frame alerts readers to the fact that Jesus knows that the lawyer is laying a trap for him to itemize a program of how to ensure eternal life for himself—evidence that Jesus is blaspheming by setting himself up as a god.

Similarly, *Old Man*'s central event, Santiago's three days sailing on the Gulf Stream, has an independent meaning as the old fisherman struggles with the forces of nature. That struggle acquires significant social meanings when Santiago's conversations with Manolin are added to the beginning and end of the fishing tale. Without the framing conversations Santiago's returning to shore with the mutilated carcass seems to be an act expected of a fisherman: if you are born to fish, as Santiago claims he was, then you catch fish, kill them and return to harbor with your catch. The conversational frame, however, establishes a relationship between Manolin and Santiago that makes Santiago's act of returning with the marlin's carcass explode with significance. It would be reasonable to expect that, given Santiago's repeated statements of love for the marlin, his exclamations on its beauty and nobility, and his identifications with it as his brother, Santiago would release the marlin's ragged, shark-gnawed remains and allow it a respectful sea burial. He carries the desecrated creature to shore, however, for people to sacrilegiously gawk at and for ignorant tourists to misidentify.

The frame reveals three motives behind Santiago's refusal to behave nobly and release the marlin at sea with a dignified valediction or elegy. First, Santiago wishes to reestablish himself as a fisherman to be reckoned with and respected by his fellow fishermen. The narrative frame pointedly tells that many younger fishermen have made fun of Santiago when Manolin treats him to a beer at the Terrace. The narrative records that Santiago "was not angry" at being made fun of, but by returning with the carcass he exhibits his skill and prowess to the disparaging young fishermen. Likewise, at the Terrace the older fishermen "looked at him and were sad. But they did not show it and they spoke politely about the current" (11). To them Santiago is an object of pity, and their sadness reflects their judgment that he is a has-been. The marlin's carcass shows these older fishermen that Santiago disdains their pity, asserts his superiority, and demands that they look at him anew—with awe and not pity.

Second, Santiago wants to reestablish himself as Manolin's tutor. As the opening paragraph of the frame makes clear, after 40 fishless days Manolin's parents conclude that Santiago is unlucky and order Manolin to fish with a different fisherman. Inasmuch as Manolin first came to fish with Santiago when he was only five years old, withdrawing him as Santiago's apprentice or pupil is not inconsequential, especially considering Santiago's lack of family and intimate friends. By returning to shore with the marlin's carcass, then, Santiago reestablishes his credentials as fisherman par excellence, under whose tutelage Manolin should fish. Santiago's status is doubly confirmed by the information he extracts from Manolin in the novella's endframe: when he asks what Manolin and his fisherman caught, Manolin confesses they caught a mere four fish, "One the first day. One the second and two the third" (124). Manolin adds no qualifiers, indicating that the four he and his fisherman caught were but small fry when compared to Santiago's giant. In addition, Santiago's return with the carcass also mocks Manolin's father's nearsightedness, as if to say, "Just how big a fish, brother, must I bring in for you to *see* how superior I am to any other fisherman into whose boat you would order your son?"

The third motive behind Santiago's choice to return to shore with the marlin's carcass is to allow Manolin to resolve his dilemma of whether to continue to obey his father or to declare his discipleship to Santiago. The narrative does not identify Manolin's age, but his thoughtfulness and concern for Santiago suggest that he is between 10 and 15 years old. He is at least old enough so that if he abandons his filial duty to his father, he will not be retrieved by force of law. When Manolin asserts in the endframe, "Now we will fish together again," Santiago merely asks, "What will your family say?" To that Manolin answers, "I do not care" (125).

In the opening frame Manolin is still an irresolute young boy, expressing his wish to fish again with Santiago. The old man acknowledges the boy's wish but tells him to stay with the boat and fisherman his father has ordered him to, saying that it is a lucky boat. When Manolin protests that he and Santiago have fished their way out of an 87-day luckless skein before, Santiago assures him, "I know you did not leave me because you doubted" (10). When Manolin places the blame on his father's orders, Santiago again accepts that father's action as "quite normal," which draws Manolin's criticism of his father, "He hasn't much faith." To that Santiago agrees, asserting "But we have," and asking "Haven't we?" (11). Manolin answers "Yes" and then promptly changes the topic, asking if he can buy Santiago a beer at the Terrace.

This conversation reveals Santiago's third motive in returning with the carcass. Although Manolin claims to have faith in Santiago, his obedience to his father shows him unwilling to act on that faith, regardless of the outcome. In the story's opening frame, then, Manolin pays only lip service to his faith in Santiago, but when Manolin sees the beached skeleton and his weary old tutor, all indecisiveness vanishes. The endframe shows him propelled into manhood, giving orders, taking charge of the situation as any true believer would of his or her injured leader.

The frame, then, adds a social dimension to Santiago's three-day fishing ordeal. It discloses the motives behind Santiago's return with the marlin's carcass: he needs to be recognized by his fellow fishermen as a professional, thereby ensuring his occupational identity as a productive member of his economy; he needs to be recognized by others as a teacher of youth, thereby confirming his social identity as a service-minded benefactor to his community; and he needs to be recognized by Manolin as a parent figure deserving of his affiliation, thereby fulfilling in sublimated form his identity as adoptive father to misguided son.

Readers may well be skeptical of the three motives I assign to Santiago's act of returning to shore with that carcass. The text never once shows him admitting to these motives. In fact, the motives seem at odds with the simplicity of a character who appears too unworldly or unintellectual to be concerned about what others think of him or too benevolent to consider forcing Manolin's discipleship. But the opening frame reveals one more piece of significant information: Santiago enjoys games of pretence. The make-believe of the pot of yellow rice with fish, the cast net, the lottery ticket, the supper he claims to have already eaten, or the washing he claims to have done before he takes supper show Santiago to be skilled in concealing reality from himself and others. If he pretends that he has a pot of yellow rice with fish, he can pretend that he gives no thought to returning to shore with the mutilated carcass. The frame, then, alerts readers to Santiago's habit of pretending.

To examine that habit more closely, consider the conversation that takes place between Santiago and Manolin while Santiago drinks his beer at the Terrace. Manolin offers to get sardines and fresh baits for the morning. Santiago claims that he has salted today's baits and will use them again. Manolin asks permission to get him four fresh baits. Santiago agrees to let him get one, whereupon Manolin insists on two, to which Santiago agrees, asking, however, "You didn't steal them?" Manolin declares, "I would," then admits, "But I bought these" (13). In this last exchange the two switch from saying what they *would* like to do, to using past tense. Instead of asking, "You won't steal them?," Santiago asks, "You didn't steal them?," and instead of declaring, "But I will buy these," Manolin declares, "But I bought these." This switch from future tense to past tense indicates that both Santiago and Manolin know that Manolin already has bought the two baits before they begin their conversation. Their conversation is a routine game of pretence, a predictable ritual. Like the fiction of the pot of yellow rice and fish, perhaps "they went through [this] fiction every day," too (16).

This little habit seems innocuous, of course. It is the kind of routine that spouses, siblings, or intimate friends often develop. But in a short masterwork where every episode must structurally function and affect the text's meanings, the conversation reveals that in small things as in large Santiago's actions can be deceptive—that like his statements, they need careful decoding. Readers who take Santiago at face value may be duped by him: he may go through several fictions every day.

THE CHARACTER-CONTRADICTING FLASHBACKS

A flashback introduces a past episode into the sequence of events in a fiction's central narrative. Usually that structural break functions comparatively—to invite consideration of some before-and-after perspective or cause-and-effect connection between the flashback and the central narrative. Two detailed flashbacks, presented as memories, interrupt *Old Man*'s fishing narrative—Santiago's arm-wrestling match with the "great negro from Cienfuegos" and his recall of the mated marlin his fishing separated. As with the novella's frame, the flashbacks also undermine Santiago's identity as benevolent brother or humble fisherman.

The Arm-Wrestling Episode

Santiago recalls the arm-wrestling episode, the narrator notes, "to give himself more confidence" (68–69). Certainly Santiago needs a confidence boost at sunset of the second day with the fish on his line. After all, his left hand has cramped, and the marlin has risen out of the ocean and intimidated him with its 18-foot length and baseball-bat-long and rapier-tapered sword. The recall of his 24-hour match of strength, will, and endurance against the "great negro from Cienfuegos" surely emboldens Santiago's resolve to endure and to vanquish his opponent in this contest too. This flashback invites consideration as a before-and-after perspective: as a young man, Santiago enjoyed singlehanded competitive contests; as an old man he continues to enjoy them.

Santiago's pleasure in competition, however, is at odds with his attitude of fraternal benevolence. A fraternal ethic commits him to altruistic cooperation with and service to others as his brother's keeper; a competitive ethic commits him to egotism—besting rivals who challenge his claims or status as his brother's superior.

The skeptical reader must distrust those who subscribe to both a fraternal and a competitive ethic at the same time and fail to acknowledge the presence of both in themselves. Santiago is subject to the charge of unwitting hypocrisy or of a double standard that lets him apply one standard one moment and the other the next. This flashback, then, registers Santiago's lack of discernment, for he equates his competitive arm-wrestling episode of the past with his allegedly fraternal contest with the marlin in the present. The competition displayed in the flashback also implies the conclusion suggested in the frame—that Santiago's relationships with fellow fishermen, Manolin's father, and Manolin himself are based on the competitive ethic of egotism rather than the cooperative ethic of altruism.

The arm-wrestling flashback further reveals Santiago's taste for self-glorification. He enjoyed being known as *El Campéon*. It gratified him to be respected for the strength of his arm and the confidence of his spirit. He relished the 24-hour spotlight, the importance of fresh referees, the tension of gamblers coming in and out all night, the changing odds, the blood that oozed from the fingernails of the wrestlers' clenched hands, the high chairs on which bettors sat against the bright blue walls, the feeding of rum to and lighting of cigarettes for his opponent, the return of his own hand from three inches off balance, the great athletic ability of his adversary, the worry of calling the match a draw because of the nearing workday, and the victory. Indelibly pictured in Santiago's memory, these details show him indulging in the memory of his glory days, an indulgence that is strangely at odds with the picture the text tries to convey of Santiago as a humble man who allegedly "had attained humility" that was neither disgraceful nor bore any "loss of true pride" (13–14). Santiago equates these two disparate experiences because they benefit hugely his reputation. His return with the marlin will all but guarantee a resurrection of his nickname, the champion. If the wish to once again be a champion were not behind this flashback, then Santiago should register some sense of disgust or amusement at the youthful foolery of arm wrestling, at the aggressive competition it promotes, or at the vanity of desiring to be known as "champ." Instead Santiago recalls only his reasons for terminating his arm-wrestling matches: he knew that beating anyone was simply a matter of whether "he wanted to badly enough and he decided that it was bad for his right hand for fishing" (70–71). No self-perception is evident of any difference between himself as a young and old man.

The Marlin-Separating Episode
The flashback of "the saddest thing" Santiago ever saw—his separating a female marlin from her

mate by catching and killing her—discloses yet another contradiction in Santiago's character. The episode records his compassion and respect for the male marlin: he stays with his mate during her "panic-stricken, despairing fight"; he circles with her as Santiago brings her boatside; he remains by her side while Santiago gaffs, clubs, and hoists her aboard with Manolin's help; and then he leaps high into the air for one last glimpse of his mate before plunging deep into the ocean: "He was beautiful, the old man remembered, and he had stayed" (50). Hard on the heels of this recall, Santiago thinks about the marlin on the far end of his fishing line, "moving steadily toward whatever he had chosen," a choice made necessary, he acknowledges, by his own "treachery."

Between his compassion and respect for the marlin on one hand and his sense of treachery on the other, Santiago shows an endearing capacity for genuine sensitivity and sentiment. He does not take lightly his conquests of the ocean's creatures.

Yet if he has such tender feelings toward these noble marlin, why does he continue to fish for them? Why doesn't he fish for smaller fry, for quantities of tuna or dolphin or porpoise or whatever else brings a good price at market, rather than for a day's single big fish? The daily dilemma of wanting to catch noble fish and of feeling that every catch is an act of betrayal and treachery reveals a man whose psychological confusion goes beyond mere hypocrisy. By anthropomorphizing the marlin of both the flashback and the central story, Santiago shows his inability to come to terms with his identity as killer and his need to continually apologize to creatures to whom he feels compelled to attribute human traits. At the least he is a mixed-up human being, not a sage old man.

Worse, Santiago's recall of this earlier episode shows that he is a sentimentalist, someone who assigns unwarranted or excessive emotions to people, creatures, or objects. His sentimentality is evident in the domestic drama he finds in the episode. He is certain that the female's companion is her mate and that the mate stays close by her because of their bond of love and sympathy. The mate circles beside the reeled-in female, presumably out of grief, and once she is harpooned, boated, and clubbed to death, he leaps high out of the water for a glimpse of his never-to-be-seen-again spouse. In other words, Santiago interprets the mating habits of the marlin as if they were like humans or, better, like geese, who mate for life. Presumably, an old and experienced fisherman should know the truth about the marlin's relationships, but in fact he does not. The marlin's mating habits have nothing in common with human or goose mating. According to David Grobecker, director of the Pacific Game Fish Research Foundation in Kona, Hawaii, marlin do not mate for life. Female marlin are broadcast spawners with multiple mates, and several males routinely swim in company with a female who spawns three to five times in a two-year period. Professor Grobecker acknowledges it is likely that the so-called mate of Santiago's hooked female may be a female marlin that follows the hooked female out of curiosity, circles out of perplexity at the hooked female's odd behavior, and leaps out of the water in puzzlement, not grief or farewell. By interpreting the "mate's" behavior according to some human drama that does not apply to marlin, Santiago's sentimentalization of the episode shows him projecting his own self-pity onto it: he feels sorrow for the bereft "mate" whose loss of his "spouse" mirrors Santiago's loneliness and wish for companionship.

By calling the episode "the saddest thing he ever saw with them" (50), Santiago further reveals his sentimentality. His use of the superlative *saddest* indicates that he has seen many sad things with marlin and this tops them all. But can this truly be the saddest of them? Although I am no deep-sea fisherman, I can readily imagine a number of fishing episodes that would give me greater sadness than Santiago's trumped-up domestic drama—catching a marlin that is so grossly malformed because of some underwater battle with predators that it is repugnant to bring to boatside or harbor; catching an aged marlin whose flesh is fungus-ridden and blotchy with disease and decay; reeling in a gut-hooked marlin that suffers great agony before being boated because the hook has not caught in the bony part of the mouth; playing a marlin so amateurishly that predatory sharks attack and mutilate it before it can be boated and while it has no chance to defend itself against its assailants. Any of these scenes would rival, if not exceed, the sadness of Santiago's flashback, for his catch of the female marlin is relatively quick and its death is merciful. The sadness of the episode reflects Santiago's emotional identification with the presumably lonely mate, an identification whose self-pity distorts the facts of the actual event. If Santiago were a more intelligent or self-perceptive man, he might be bemused by his sentimentality, find it embarrassing, or at least distance himself from his judgment that the flashback with the marlin "mates" was "the saddest thing he ever saw with them."

To call Santiago a sentimentalist may be an inaccurate and simplistic reading of him, for his habit of repeating his family fantasies—identifying the creatures of his world as brothers—may be a symptom of a neurotic obsession. That obsession suggests that, unable to view his relationship with nature as either a Darwinian "survival of the fittest" or a harmonic integration in some overarching and unfathomable mystery, Santiago needs to read his encounters with marlin in fraternal terms because of a deep incapacity to reconcile himself to his role as killer of nature's creatures. Rather than face that killing role, he tries to compensate by spraying the mist of fraternalism over his fishing activities. As with the flashback of the "great negro from Cienfuegos," so too here: this recall of his betrayal of the marlin's "mate" shows that Santiago does not develop or grow from his experiences. He gains no wisdom between the earlier catch and this one of the giant marlin. Both flashbacks show him fixated to the same attitudes now as he had then, for he registers no self-reflection or self-consciousness—no sense of dismay at, or disapproval of, his conduct or thoughts about either flashback.

So again, whether measuring Santiago by the novella's idealization or by its structure, I find that his feet are made of clay. But instead of mourning over a Santiago who is stripped of his nobility by skeptical readings, I hope to lead readers to new insights about him—to perspectives on his character that enrich the novella by displaying his layered ambiguities. Indeed, there is much more work to be done on Santiago's character, as the following chapter shows.

6

Character

THE CLAIM OF STRANGENESS

Both Santiago and the narrator speak of the old man's strangeness. "I am a strange old man" (14), Santiago declares to Manolin at the Terrace, where the boy has bought him a beer, and on the second day of his contest with the marlin Santiago reminds himself that "I told the boy I was a strange old man. . . . Now is when I must prove it" (66). The narrator remarks Santiago's "strange shoulders" and his hands' deep-creased scars, as "old as erosions in a fishless desert" (10). Other qualities seem to mark him as someone who conducts himself according to an extraordinary set of standards—his claim to have once been able to "see quite well in the dark" (67); his empathy with the fish he kills as "our true brothers"; his identification with "the stars that are my brothers" (77); and his dreams of lions on the beaches of Africa. Certainly his conquest of the giant marlin seems to indicate that he is exceptional—a rare and strange old man.

If Santiago is strange in the sense of "exceptionally good," he should provide a model of idealized behavior that invites imitation and emulation. Unfortunately, as discussed in earlier chapters, his questionable fraternalism, his self-serving motives for returning to harbor with the marlin's mutilated carcass, and the self-glorifying or sentimentalizing flashbacks all portray him as a morally flawed mortal. His killing of the marlin, identifications with lions and Joe DiMaggio, and notions of professionalism, paternalism, and environmentalism are not strange. Readers who follow where those actions lead discover that Santiago shows quite a normal range of common human ambitions and confusions.

THE KILLING OF THE MARLIN

The clearest evidence of Santiago's common confusions is his killing of the marlin. For despite his skill, patience, endurance, and declarations of love for and brotherhood with the marlin, rolling the marlin on its side and plunging his harpoon into its heart is neither intelligent nor strange. The act cannot be blamed on mental and physical fatigue, for Santiago has had three days to think about the killing and its consequences.

Santiago reveals his lack of intelligence by failing to anticipate the results of his killing of the marlin. It jumps on the afternoon of the second day, displaying its length, which Santiago calculates as two feet longer than his skiff, so he knows that there is no way to boat this fish and he will have to lash the marlin beside his skiff, making it vulnerable to predators. Further, he acknowledges near sunset of the second day that his contest could be jeopardized by sharks: "If sharks come God pity him and me" (68). He also knows that to kill the marlin requires harpooning it, which will spill blood into the ocean currents, telegraphing to sharks an invitation to dinner. If Santiago were intelligent, he would at least wrestle with the dilemma of how to kill the marlin without any bloodletting, or he would show some overt sign that he is aware of bloodletting's calamitous consequences. Finally, knowing that he is ill equipped to defend the marlin against shark attacks, an intelligent Santiago would have avoided harpooning it at all costs.

Santiago's killing of the marlin better suggests partly concealed motives for killing it. The earlier discussion of frame and flashbacks emphasized the motives of self-vindication, revenge, and self-glorification, but Santiago also has a private motive that again reveals his ambition and not strangeness: that motive is self-validation—the need to prove himself.

Often we voluntarily put ourselves in test situations—physical, mental, emotional, moral, academic, and so on—to find out whether we can perform under pressure. We often find ourselves faced with trying circumstances that test our character, as well. More often, we fantasize about such experiences, imagining how we would conduct ourselves if confronted by them, or we remember experiences in which we have not conducted ourselves well and think of better things to say or do. Such experiences are vital to the maturing process and to self-esteem, for they let us measure our development and assess our self-imposed standards of conduct. Nevertheless, it is important to differentiate between experiences that prove our worth to ourselves and those that prove our worth to others. The former—genuinely self-validating experiences—are valuable because they require us to prove our worth neither at another's expense nor to impress another. The latter—tainted self-validating experiences—characterize Santiago's killing of the marlin.

After the marlin leaps into the air the first time and Santiago's left hand cramps badly, he resolves that he will kill the marlin "In all his greatness and his glory"; he admits to himself that "it is unjust. . . . But I will show him what a man can do and what a man endures" (66). Santiago's need, to "show" the marlin what he himself can do, reveals his utterly common compulsion to prove his own worth by proving his superiority to an adversary. Like many people who feel that their abilities and worth are undervalued or unrecognized, Santiago feels that he must better some adversary. A truly strange old man would not so readily, if at all, let himself be identified with such a tainted sentiment because it is one ordinarily and understandably linked to the macho notion of vaunting one's manhood before a rival. Also, Santiago slips into the common confusion of anthropomorphizing his nonhuman adversary so as to visualize the combat in human rather than in natural terms. It is doubtful that Santiago's marlin has the mental ability to applaud Santiago's superior performance, yet, like many a hunter, Santiago assigns such intelligence to his prey, projecting onto it his psychological need for a personalized drama that has no verifiable reality in the prey's mind.

Santiago further taints his potentially self-validating ordeal with the marlin by declaring, immediately after he thinks he must show the fish what he can do, "I told the boy I was a strange old man. . . . Now is when I must prove it (66). Here he discloses that besting the fish to prove his worth to it and himself is insufficient; he also must prove his worth to the boy. Santiago's compulsion to win admiration in another's eyes shows ambition for approval or social commendation. Add to this his resolve to prove to the boy that his actions amount to strangeness and, abruptly, Santiago's actions during the three-day episode tarnish. His need to show himself extraordinary removes his conduct from the category of self-validation and puts it into the category of the arm-wrestling flashback—a self-glorifying power trip.

Were Santiago truly a strange old man, he would not need to kill the fish. A stranger man might have engaged in some form of catch-and-release fishing. After all, Santiago validates himself by proving his prowess and dominance when he brings the marlin to boatside and rolls it on its side, ready for the harpoon. A strange man, gratified with the combat, might then have cut the line and let the fish drift away, even if to its death. A strange old man would have risen above the common need to have a carcass as verifiable proof of the combat; he would be indifferent to others who would jeer at his "tall" story of the giant fish he dominated but released. Moreover, a truly strange old man would have shown genuine reverence for the marlin's carcass. He would have unknotted its lashings to the skiff and allowed the once-beautiful fish the dignity of a watery grave rather than the indignity of letting its mutilated skeleton become a spectacle.

Character

THE DREAMS AND DAYDREAMS: LIONS AND DIMAGGIO

As someone who likes to imagine himself strange, Santiago indulges in the ordinary wish to be recognized as an individualist who stands out from the crowd. He thinks, for instance, "of the sea as *la mar* which is what people call her in Spanish when they love her" (29), but younger men, speak of the sea as "*el mar* which is masculine. They spoke of her as a contestant or a place or even an enemy" (30). Lesser fishermen work the water near shore; they would have quailed at being towed to sea (possibly beyond rescue or return), would have given up on that contest and the one against the marauding sharks, would have been deeply discouraged after going 84 fishless days. But not Santiago. These differences, however, can be interpreted as signs of Santiago's quite ordinary, self-serving ambition to set himself apart from his fellow man, an ambition in which Santiago has the narrator's assistance. Santiago's wish to be regarded as strange or unique is simply the utterly common ambition to gain recognition for uncommon deeds or achievements, to be deferred to as a notable or celebrity, to establish a reputation that awes beholders. His dreams and daydreams further reveal his ambition.

Santiago's memory of standing at evening on the deck of a square-rigged ship and seeing lions on the African beaches seems to indicate a beatific harmony with the natural world and its creatures. He recalls that daydream when he wishes for peace and sleep, as when he wishes, on the afternoon of the second day, that he could sleep and dream about the lions (66). When he sleeps that night he "began to dream of the long yellow beach and he saw the first of the lions come down onto it in the early dark and then the other lions came and he rested his chin on the wood of the bows where the ship lay anchored with the evening off-shore breeze and he waited to see if there would be more lions and he was happy" (81). Likewise, at novella's end he sleeps, dreaming, the narrator writes, of the lions.

The image of lions, engaged in nonpredatory activity, seems an appropriate image for Santiago to call on, consciously and uncon-sciously, if the narrator wishes to establish an alliance of strangeness between the lions and Santiago. For these unaggressive lions of Santiago's memory and dreams are as much a natural anomaly as is a fisherman with a reverentially fraternal feeling toward the natural world he preys on.

But Santiago's identification with the lions also—if not better—reveals his wish for alliance with extraordinary animals. He does not dream of monkeys, turtles, or hares strolling on an African beach: only the king of beasts will do. That choice, conscious and unconscious, betrays a desire to be associated with regal animals, to stand in the ranks of the prestigious lords of the universe, to be regarded as their equal, as one of them. Such infantile fantasies understandably swell the heads of countless egocentric youths—as well as their elders who suffer from protracted adolescence. There is little that is strange in such common delusions of grandeur, but Santiago's failure to find anything amusing or pretentious about his leonine dreaming habit suggests his blindness to the ordinariness of his self-assigned strangeness. Such blindness invites pity or even scorn rather than respect.

Equally adolescent is Santiago's daydreaming identification with the legendary New York Yankee centerfielder, "Joltin' Joe" DiMaggio. It is normal, of course, to identify with role models, to idolize exemplary athletes, superstars, or idealized career figures who spur us into emulating their deeds and philosophies, imitating their mannerisms and habits, and Santiago fixes on an appropriately aging and injured figure to identify with. As with his dreams of the lions, however, Santiago singles out another "royal" figure in DiMaggio, whose 56-consecutive-game hitting streak in 1941 is virtually an untouchable record—one that many sports fans regard as the most remarkable athletic performance of all time and one that statisticians marvel at because of the enormous odds against accomplishing it. Santiago identifies with this athletic "lord of the universe," not some lesser athlete. Santiago also thinks of Dick Sisler, who played Cuban winter baseball in 1945–46. His four home runs in two days—one a 500-foot shot, the first ever hit out of Havana's ballpark—instantly catapulted him into Cuban stardom.[20]

Santiago repeats one epithet for DiMaggio, Sisler, and the baseball managers who are mentioned in Santiago's and Manolin's opening-frame conversation (McGraw, Durocher, Luque, and Gonzalez)—great. Indeed, in a 420-word stretch (21–23) the word is used a dozen times. It may well be that Santiago uses the term to relate to Manolin's level of usage and ideas, but the conversation leads to Manolin's declaration that Santiago is "the best fisherman." When Santiago modestly denies that superlative with, "I know others better," Manolin retorts, "There are many good fishermen and some great ones. But there is only you" (23). This puts Santiago in a class by himself, which may have been Santiago's intent throughout the conversation and the litany of "greats." Whatever his intent, the conversation reveals Santiago's obsession with greatness, an ambition of countless humans who lay no claim to being strange.

PROFESSIONALISM

Just before the giant marlin strikes Santiago's baited hook, the old fisherman thinks enviously of rich fishermen whose boats have radios for listening to baseball games. He scolds himself for thinking of baseball: "Now is the time to think of only one thing. That which I was born for" (40). Ten pages later, well fastened to the towing marlin and just after he remorsefully recalls the mated marlin his fishing separated, Santiago thinks, "Perhaps I should not have been a fisherman." He immediately negates the thought with "But that was what I was born for" (50). After Santiago has defended the marlin against the Mako shark and wonders if it was sinful for him to have killed the fish, he assures himself, "You killed him for pride and because you are a fisherman" (105).

Santiago's notion of doing what he was born to do expresses an attitude common to people who believe they are called to their destiny—appointed to it by providential decree, fated to it from some chain of circumstances over which they have little if any influence, born to it through some genetic makeup that allows no opportunity for change or choice. This attitude is fatalistic when people regard themselves as victims, but it is religious or philosophic in people who congratulate themselves for having been chosen to fulfill some mission or who pride themselves on their occupation. This last is the case with Santiago, for his conviction that he was born to be a fisherman expresses pride in his profession.

There is moral confusion in the professional's belief or claim that "I was born" to be anything, whether outfitter or soldier, lawyer or logger, politician or entertainer, doctor or factory worker, bureaucrat or teacher, corporate executive or supermarket cashier, football coach or newspaper reporter. The confusion lies in the assumption that professionals must measure their occupational actions according to standards that differ from those they use to measure their normal actions. This assumption implies that a professional's double standards differ from those criticized as ethically dubious, if not specious. They do not differ. All double-standard systems inequitably or arbitrarily assign one set of standards to one class of people or events and another set to a different class of people or events. The purpose of such double standards is to privilege oneself at the expense of others or to legitimize illegitimate, harmful, prejudicial, or discriminatory actions.

Certainly there are differences among the foregoing list of professionals. Some occupations require considerably more training, intelligence, and responsibility than others, but all occupations primarily require of their members the skill to perform professional tasks efficiently and ethically. The assumption that professionals must march to the beat of two drummers—one professional, one human—is a rationalization invoked to justify ethically dubious behavior. There are many examples of how people use allegiances to professional principles, expectations, or conventions to excuse or exonerate their behavior—the coach who bends recruiting rules in the name of building a title-contending team; the entertainer who borrows another's material or routines in the name of perfecting flawed work; the doctor who withholds information vital to a patient's right of informed consent in the name of expediting a treatment program; the executive who suborns his inferiors in the name of seizing an edge on the marketplace; the politician who accepts corporate gratuities in the name of legislative investigation or constituent services; the bureaucrat who disallows any exceptions to policies in the name of equity; the factory worker who willfully meets only minimum production quotas in the name of contractual stipulations; the teacher who quantifies all student work and assigns grades according to a strict bell curve in the name of objectivity; the soldier who violates laws by obeying his military superiors in the name of a higher patriotism; the logger who clearcuts stands of timber in the name of improved reforestation; or the outfitter who guides hunters to big game in the name of thinning oversized herds and protecting the environment from overgrazing.

When professional principles run counter to humanitarian principles of consideration for the rights and claims of nature or of other people, the professional's claim to be doing what he or she "was born for" is simply a rationalization for egotism: "I want to do this for personal reasons, but I'll disguise it as a professional necessity required of me."

Santiago's confused professionalism is his rationale for killing the marlin: in fact, the text invites measuring Santiago's action as that of a professional fisherman and not as an ethical human. That is, Santiago continually expresses sharply ambivalent feelings toward his hooked marlin, respecting its nobility, beauty, and strangeness (48, 67, 84) but still vowing to kill it. This conflict between feelings of affiliation and aggression reflects an authentic ethical dilemma. Santiago could resolve it by letting his humanitarian principles prevail: he could simply respect his "brother" and release him rather than commit the act of fratricide. As a professional, however, Santiago confusedly believes that he must kill the marlin, for he was born to fish and to fish requires killing, he thinks. In other words, Santiago rationalizes his aggressive act by believing that his act of killing is not an act of killing if he can disguise it as a professional act. Such subterfuge, even if not consciously committed, is a game of verbal substitution that Santiago lacks the intelligence to see through, a form of hypocrisy that he fails to understand, a confusion that he never bothers to sort out.

Like many professionals, then, Santiago views himself as an expert, someone so highly knowledgeable in his "line of work" that a layperson's questions or concerns are beside the point. But the ethical layperson asks the doctor whether her professional training provides her with the medical resources, detailed information, and technical proficiency to administer her skills only to insured patients or whether it teaches her to be a healer entrusted with ensuring human health to all patients in her society. Likewise, the ethical layperson asks the lawyer whether his professional education equips him to manipulate the laws, precedents, and loopholes to the advantage of his paying client or whether it equips him to be a guardian of a society of laws and justice that privileges no client. So, too, the ethical layperson asks Santiago, the professional who was born to be a fisherman, whether his training and experience prepared him to be an expert and methodical killer of fish, whose watery kingdom he daily tries to plunder (however sanctimoniously or apologetically) or whether they prepared him to be a trustee of a vulnerable sanctuary whose resources may not be indefinitely renewable, a fishery whose species may be jeopardized by the predatory fisherman.

PATERNALISM

As the skeptical reading of Santiago's return with the marlin's carcass earlier explained, one of the old man's motives is to win back his role as Manolin's tutor, and Santiago's resolve to prove to the boy his status as a "strange old man" further shows the importance to Santiago of Manolin's discipleship. Given not only Santiago's benevolent feelings toward Manolin but also the boy's reciprocal respect as well as the energy and knowledge and time Santiago has already committed to Manolin's education, the old fisherman's role as Manolin's substitute father seems deserved. Yet Santiago's actions are paternalistic, further eroding his claim to strangeness and revealing his commonness.

Paternalism is the label assigned to a person or group's coercive or manipulative actions that consciously or unconsciously interfere with an individual or group's exercise of self-rule, or autonomy. The moral justification customarily used in defense of paternalistic acts is that they benefit, or are in the best interests of, the person being coerced or manipulated. They have particular legitimacy in cases of individuals or groups who need protection because of diminished autonomy—mentally ill or disabled people, the elderly suffering from memory loss or senility, and children. Many paternalistic acts, however, wrong a supposed beneficiary by routinely withholding or manipulating information necessary to an individual or group. That violates two moral principles—informed consent, which acknowledges individuals' right to full information and participation in decisions affecting themselves, and respect for people, which recognizes the dignity or intrinsic worth of individuals and mandates respect for their autonomy. Parents routinely interfere with children's activities, and doctors and families withhold information from terminally ill persons, assuming that such information will harm the person.

Santiago's paternalism is not as overtly coercive as is Manolin's father's: Manolin insists that after 40 fishless days, "It was papa made me leave. I am a boy and I must obey him" (10). In contrast Santiago exercises no coercive force over Manolin. He does not try to persuade Manolin to fish with him on the eighty-fifth day, nor does he, on his return, overtly pressure Manolin into making a pledge of discipleship. His paternalism is nevertheless manipulative, perhaps unwittingly so. Neither before he sails out nor after he returns does Santiago admit to Manolin that his struggles will be or were to prove to Manolin that he was "a strange old man." Inasmuch as he acknowledges his motive aloud when battling the marlin, his withholding it on his return may partly explain Manolin's prompt pledge, "we will fish together now for I still have much to learn" (125). Further, battered as Santiago is, his declaration, "I missed you," and his comment that the sharks "beat me" (124) play strongly on Manolin's sympathy and guilt, influencing his ready discipleship.

Santiago's fishing skills during his three-day ordeal seem to reveal his superiority to other tutors available to Manolin, but his actions also show his determination, at all costs, to win Manolin's discipleship. That reveals his unexpressed conviction that he knows what is best for Manolin and his unacknowledged commitment to influence Manolin's taking the voluntary act to break free from his own father's governance and to affiliate himself with Santiago. By acting on this moral principle of "beneficence"—choosing actions likely to result in a balance of benefits over harms—Santiago seems well intentioned, for he thinks that Manolin's welfare will be best served by a closer affiliation than they have had, but his paternalistic actions harmfully manipulate Manolin's sympathy and guilt: he infringes on Manolin's autonomy, causing him to commit himself to a course of action while under emotional and psychological stress.

Further, neither on his return nor during the ordeal, when he repeated his wish that Manolin were with him, does Santiago think about the consequences that Manolin's pledge of discipleship will generate. Others will be affected by the decision he influences Manolin into making. Although Manolin's discipleship may be in his own and Santiago's best interests, it harms Manolin's family. Given the strong patriarchal values of Santiago's culture, Manolin's father will surely suffer at least embarrassment among his fellow fisherman, and perhaps social disgrace, when his loss of authority over his son becomes known. His loss may even have a financial cost, for at novella's end he is deprived of a son to hire out to a needful fisherman, a son whose contribution to the family's earning power will likely be redirected. Moreover, Santiago's paternalistic influence on Manolin's decision to affiliate himself with Santiago also harms the nearly blind old fisherman with whom Manolin has fished the past 48 days. He must now find a new helper or apprentice to whom he must teach the routines of his fishing. Finally, Manolin's impetuous pledge to Santiago may harm himself by causing his community to regard his discipleship an act of filial treachery to his parents, possibly causing him some measure of ostracism. These consequences of Manolin's pledge are unspecified in the novella, but their textual absence does not negate or nullify their reality. Part of the richness of Hemingway's novella lies in the issues it propels into readers' considerations, even those not anchored to fact.

Were Santiago less morally confused, less self-interested, more ethically astute and genuinely concerned that Manolin commit no act injurious to others or himself, then the old man's deeds would merit moral approval. Their paternalism merits moral disapproval, however, and yet esthetic appreciation, for their rich complexity adds resonance and depth to Santiago's character.

ENVIRONMENTALISM

After Santiago recalls his separation of the mated marlin, he evaluates the episode as "the saddest thing I ever saw with them" (50). His superlative "saddest" indicates that he has seen many sad scenes with marlin, and his many expressions of empathy for the giant marlin further show that Santiago routinely grieves over the marlin he catches. That grief swells into remorse this time. Santiago is "sorry that he killed the fish"(103), wishes he "had never hooked the fish," feels that "perhaps it was a sin to kill the fish," and rationalizes that "if you love him, it's not a sin to kill him" (105). After the marlin is quite mutilated by the rapacious pair of *galanos*, Santiago apologizes several times to it: "I'm sorry, fish" (110).

That Santiago can respond with so much emotional anguish to his act seems to speak well of him as a man whose occupation has not blunted his sensitivity or hardened him against the natural creatures on whom his livelihood depends. But Santiago's remorse and emotional anguish expose his failure to resolve his ambivalence toward his exploitative trade. On one hand, fishing is his profession, what he was born for, a trade that requires the death of his prey; on the other hand, he suffers from his constant treachery to that prey, whose capture subjects him to many saddening experiences. His remorse for his treachery should have brought him long before to some resolution of this conflict between his professionalism and his fraternalism. One course of action for a sensitive, intelligent and ethically responsible human whose emotions guide his actions would be to jettison his proud professionalism and embrace some form of environmentalism.

To an environmentalist, nature's laws, creatures, processes, and ecological systems demand respectful safeguarding, both to preserve earth's species and to maintain balance in the ecological hierarchies so vital to earth's continued existence. Santiago's remorse over the noble victims of his fishing suggests a glimmering awareness that there could be something more important to him than the productivity ethic of catch, kill, and sell—some principle more in harmony with nature than the mercantilistic practice of harvest and market. Like many a person raised in a capitalistic culture—where survival presumably depends on competition, conquest, and commerce—Santiago cannot think his way out of a cash consciousness to recognize that his profession disables him from coming to a sense of serene harmony with his natural surroundings. Much less does Santiago show any glimpse that his fishery may be a depletable resource or that he may have some responsibility to its conservation or renewal. For all his professed and portrayed beneficence, he plunders nature's bounty, as oblivious as his fellow fishermen to any obligation to be a trustee of its renewal, guarantor of its welfare, or spokesperson for laws to ensure its survival for future generations of environmentally sensitive fishermen, once again showing his lack of transcendent wisdom and revealing his self-centered preoccupations. In so doing, he continues to emerge from behind his initial mask of benevolent saintliness as a quite ordinary human, one whose muddled confusions provide perspectives from which readers can see themselves.

Were Santiago an exemplary and strange old man, Hemingway could have had him come to some recognition as a result of his ordeal. After all, Hemingway's narrator insists that after harpooning the marlin "the old man looked carefully into the glimpse of vision that he had" (94). Some eventual dramatization of the substance of that vision should be presented, but none is forthcoming—or at least no vision shows Santiago ennobled by his experience. A theological vision might show to him that his killing of the noble marlin was truly a sin against God's creation, a theocidal act for which forgiveness and penance would require an end to his fishing; a psychological vision would show that his killing was a fratricidal act committed against both the fish and those who feign brotherhood with him but betray him with abandonment (Manolin) or disdain (Manolin's father and the ridiculing fishermen); an ethical vision would show that his act exposes self-serving motives that he tries to conceal behind the masks of professionalism and paternalism; or an environmental vision might show that his act was a symbolic violation of the rights of the natural world to be unexploited by a profiteering trade that greedily rapes the seas, a trade with which Santiago is in naive collusion.

Any of these visions could lead Santiago, at the very least, to explain to Manolin his decision to give up his lifelong profession and thereby put an end to the emotional self-torture his killing of marlin causes him. Better, he could declare his intent to take up some occupation—mending or making fishing nets, say—free from the profit-inspired accumulation of wealth or from the temptation to continually engage in the vaingloriousness of proving himself in others' eyes to be a strange old man. Best, his vision could lead him to some self-recognition. He could acknowledge himself to be an ordinary man, plagued by common ambitions and confusions, not an exemplary man whose conduct or beliefs Manolin should imitate or emulate.

That Hemingway denies Santiago the ability or opportunity to articulate any of these visions or self-recognitions is a credit to his novella. Any one of them would resolve the text one-dimensionally by emphasizing one thematic chord to the exclusion of others. By leaving Santiago's vision undefined, Hemingway allows readers to read it positively and negatively, to assign to Santiago's experience the vision—or lack of vision—that best suits their pluralistic interpretations of his character.

7

Style

In the eyes of the Nobel Prize Committee, with *The Old Man and the Sea* Hemingway produced "a work of ideal tendencies," a primary criterion for the award. The citation also remarked the "heroic pathos" of his fiction, his "manly love of danger and adventure," and his "natural admiration for every individual who fights the good fight in a world of reality overshadowed by violence and death." Central to Hemingway's receiving the award was his "powerful style-making mastery of the art of modern narrative." Although his narrative mastery has not often been singled out for special praise, his stylistic mastery has. Indeed, he is best known for the apparent simplicity of his language and sentence structure as well as his studied avoidance of verbal ornamentation. His so-called clean, lucid prose has presumably schooled more than one generation of American writers.

Yet this novella is not an instance of Hemingway's style at its best. Certainly the narrative has its excellences. Hemingway deftly begins his narrative at a suspenseful point: on the eve of the eighty-fifth day will this old fisherman push his weary and unlucky body to sea again? In the foreground of the narrative Santiago battles with marlin and sharks; in the background memories vie with necessary exposition and Santiago's thoughts on different sea creatures and episodes. The excitement of Santiago's finally bringing the marlin to boatside, and, later, the pathos of his valiantly trying to beat off the marauding sharks show Hemingway's narrative skill in engaging readers' emotional participation in Santiago's ordeal. Hemingway's stylistic power modulates sentences with rhythms and visual images so that they read like poetic vignettes. One nearly flawless passage (that I will return to later) produces poetic cadences with its dominant four-beat lines:

```
        /   x  /  x  x   /
1    Just before it was dark,

        x  x   /  x  x  / x  x x  / x   /
2    as they passed a great island of Sargasso weed

        x    /   x    /   x x  /    /
3    that heaved and swung in the light sea

        x   /   x  / x   x   / x   /
4    as though the ocean were making love

        x   /   x   / x x / x   /   x
5    with something under a yellow blanket,

        x   /   /  x  / x  x x  / x
6    his small line was taken by a dolphin.

        x /  x /   x  x   /  x x  /
7    He saw it first when it jumped in the air,

        /   /  x x   /  x x  /
8    true gold in the last of the sun

        x   /  x  x  /  x  / x x x  /
9    and bending and flapping wildly in the air.

        x   /  x  /  x x  /
10   It jumped again and again

        x x  / x / x  x x  /
11   in the acrobatics of its fear

        x  x   /   x  x   /  x x   /
12   and he worked his way back to the stern

        x   /  x  x  / x  x  /  /
13   and crouching and holding the big line

        x  x  /   /   x  /
14   with his right hand and arm,
```

```
      x   /   x   /  x   /   x  x   /    x
15  he pulled the dolphin in with his left hand,

     /   x   x x    /    /    x   /
16  stepping on the gained line each time

     x   x   /   /  /
17  with his bare left foot.

      x  x  /   x   / x   /
18  When the fish was at the stern,

      /  x   x   /  x   x   /  x  /  x  x  x / x
19  plunging and cutting from side to side in desperation,

     x   /   /    x    / x  x   /
20  the old man leaned over the stern

     x   /  x x    /    x   /  /
21  and lifted the burnished gold fish

      x  x   /  x   /   / x  x   /
22  with its purple spots over the stern.

     x   /    x    / x   x   / x  x
23  Its jaws were working convulsively

     x   /   /  x   /   x   /
24  in quick bites against the hook

     x  x    /   x x   / x   x x    /
25  and it pounded the bottom of the skiff

     x  x   /   x   / x x   /  x  x   /
26  with its long flat body, its tail and its head

     x x x   /    x x   /  x   / x   / x   /
27  until he clubbed it across the shining golden head

     x/  x   /  x   /   x   /
28  until it shivered and was still.
```

(72–73)

(The flaw is in line 22 where "over the stern" not only repeats the "over the stern" of line 20 but also constitutes a squinting modifier, ambiguously referring either to the boat's or the dolphin's stern.)

Despite other fine examples of such excellent paragraphs, the style in the novel is often flawed. Similes—an unusually high number for Hemingway—are often self-conscious; abstractions mar important moments; slogans lead to pretentiousness; and occasional inconsistencies and confused sentences diminish the novella's art.

Style

SIMILES

In his 1932 bullfighting treatise *Death in the Afternoon* Hemingway declares his dislike of "flowery writing." Of any writer, he says, "No matter how good a phrase or a simile he may have[,] if he puts it in where it is not absolutely necessary and irreplaceable he is spoiling his work for egotism. Prose is architecture, not interior decoration" (191). According to this criterion, Hemingway frequently spoils *Old Man* "for egotism." Noted as his early writing was for its lack of ornamental figures of speech, the novella rivals only *For Whom the Bell Tolls* for frequency of similes (and the similes in the 1940 war novel were integral to the epic design and formulas Hemingway embedded in that novel).

A number of the novella's similes are unobjectionable—the narrator's description of the marlin's sword "as long as a baseball bat and tapered like a rapier" (62) or of Santiago's patched shirt as "like the [patched] sail" (18) or of the African lions Santiago fondly remembers "play[ing] like young cats in the dusk" (25). Even some of the similes that call attention to themselves are not particularly objectionable. When Santiago "looked at the sky and saw the white cumulus built like friendly piles of ice cream" (61), the cliché is appropriate enough to Santiago's experience and imagination—as well as to his circumstances, in which a pile of ice cream would be especially welcome. The novella's first simile, which likens Santiago's flour-sack–patched sail to "the flag of permanent defeat" (9) is tolerable, even though it solicits readers' pity before they have a context for the character. Even the simile in the lengthy dolphin-catching passage I quoted above is unobjectionable, although its eroticism is not altogether in harmony with Santiago's celibacy: "they passed a great island of Sargasso weed that heaved and swung in the light sea as though the ocean were making love with something under a yellow blanket."

Other similes call unnecessary attention to themselves and reflect a writer self-consciously and inappropriately "turning on the style." The narrator, for instance, describes Santiago's cramped left hand "as tight as the gripped claws of an eagle" (63). This not only exaggerates the sinewy clutch of a cramped hand but also unsubtly insinuates another of Santiago's royal resemblances, this time to the king of birds. More arresting is the narrator's second simile, which asserts that Santiago's scars "were as old as erosions in a fishless desert" (10), polevaulting readers into a mythic or timeless landscape, prematurely suggesting that Santiago is an exemplary human before he has been dramatized in events in which he behaves extraordinarily.

Two similes are particularly offensive. One is when Santiago sees the first pair of sharks approach his boat and the narrator likens Santiago's "*Ay*" to "a noise such as a man might make, involuntarily, feeling the nail go through his hands and into the wood" (107). This simile heavy-handedly insists that readers link Santiago and Christ, an identification that Santiago's character and conduct little warrant. The other is the narrator's description of the dead marlin's eye looking "as detached as the mirrors in a periscope or as a saint in a procession" (96). The "mirrors in a periscope" is inappropriate because it introduces into the primitive world of simple fishermen a reference to the technological wizardry of twentieth-century submarine warfare. The eye's being likened to a "saint in a procession" once again imposes religious dimensions onto a natural phenomenon, steering readers to think of the marlin in the way they are steered to think of *Sant*iago—as saintly. In his earlier writings Hemingway did not spoil his text with such stylistic blunders.

ABSTRACTIONS

The previously quoted dolphin-catching episode is noteworthy for its descriptive power as well as its poetic cadences. The narrator, for instance, keeps his eye on the literal action of the dolphin. He records it jumping, bending, flapping, plunging, cutting from side to side, convulsively biting the hook, pounding, shivering—and then its stillness. Likewise he records Santiago as he works, crouches, holds, pulls, steps, leans, lifts, and clubs. He records, too, the details of the scene so that a reader sees the sunset; watches Santiago's careful movement to the stern, his left-handed hauling-in of the line, his left-footed anchoring of each gained segment of it; and sees the dolphin's flatness and burnished goldness as well as its transfer from sea to skiff bottom.

This is the kind of descriptive writing at which Hemingway excels, so enlivening a scene that readers can see and respond to it with individual judgments and emotions. It is the quality of writing found in young Nick Adams's trout fishing in "The Big Two-Hearted River," Francis Macomber's buffalo hunting in "The Short Happy Life of Francis Macomber," and Pedro Romero's bullfighting in *The Sun Also Rises*. Part of the power of such writing—of *showing* as it is commonly termed—is Hemingway's narrators' refusal to resort to abstractions that simultaneously blot visual particulars and steer emotional responses.

Such powerful descriptive writing is absent in the passage on the killing of the marlin, the climax of the novella's central story. Santiago says to himself, "Never have I seen a greater, or more beautiful, or a calmer or more noble thing than you, brother" (92), and his abstractions legitimately reveal his private, emotional assessment of the fish. When Santiago pulls the marlin onto its side next to the boat, however, the narrator writes, "He took all his *pain* and what was left of his *strength* and his long-gone *pride* and he put it against the fish's *agony*" (93; italics mine); the italicized abstractions constitute *telling* (as opposed to showing or dramatizing). They insist that the reader accept the narrator's abstractions. If the narrator described only physical actions, readers might privately assess Santiago's actions much as he does, using similar abstractions, or readers might assess them quite differently: "He took all his *ego* and what was left of his *willfulness* and his nearly gone *perseverence* and he put them against the fish's *instinctual aggression*." In brief, Hemingway's poor narration distrusts and insults readers by instructing them in how they should feel and think about this climactic moment in the novel. Good narration permits readers to make their own abstracted value judgments.

Equally objectionable is the value-laden, abstraction-heavy description of the marlin's last leap, as it "rose high out of the water, showing all his *great length* and *width* and all his *power* and his *beauty*" (94; italics mine). This passage seems to obscure whether this is a marlin or a torpedo, a natural or a man-made artifact. Compare this to the vivid description of the marlin's first leap:

> The line rose slowly and steadily and then the surface of the ocean bulged ahead of the boat and the fish came out. He came out unendingly and water poured from his sides. He was bright in the sun and his head and back were dark purple and in the sun the stripes on his sides showed wide and a light lavender. His sword was as long as a baseball bat and tapered like a rapier and he rose his full length from the water and then re-entered it, smoothly, like a diver and the old man saw the great scythe-blade of his tail go under and the line commenced to race out. (62–63)

Except for the "unendingly" the relative absence of abstractions permits readers to value the fish's power and beauty and threat as they wish—as effective narration always does.

The narrator succumbs to this practice of abstraction elsewhere, often compounding the stylistic wrong with redundancy. Consider Santiago's defense of the marlin's carcass against the Mako shark. He rams the harpoon into the shark's brain: "He hit it with his blood mushed hands driving a good harpoon with all his strength. He hit it without *hope* but with *resolution* and *complete malignancy*" (102; italics mine). The second sentence here interprets Santiago's action, the abstractions depriving readers of part of their pleasure and duty in reading fiction—to assign their own value judgments to events and characters.

Another example follows Santiago's killing of the marlin. As the silvery and still fish floats on the water, its blood spreading "like a cloud," the narrator writes that "the old man looked carefully in the glimpse of the vision that he had" (94). Here the narrator insists that readers recognize that Santiago has experienced some visionary experience, relying on the abstraction "vision" (and the adverbial emphasis on "carefully") to indicate that readers must recognize the profoundness of the experience if they wish to capture the full resonance of the narrative. The narrator repeats this abstraction four pages later, remarking that when Santiago "had seen the fish come out of the water and hang motionless in the sky before he fell, he was sure there was some *great strangeness* and he could not believe it" (98; italics mine). Here as elsewhere, the narrative strategy of employing abstractions artlessly prompts readers to find symbolic significance in them. Such an amateurish strategy is not what readers expect from Hemingway at his best.

SLOGANS

After Santiago kills the Mako shark, the largest *dentuso* he has ever seen, he regrets having hooked the marlin but consoles himself by saying aloud, "But man is not made for defeat. . . . A man can be destroyed but not defeated" (103). Earlier in the novel he tells Manolin, who assures him that he can borrow two dollars and a half to play the lottery, "I think perhaps I can too. But I try not to borrow. First you borrow. Then you beg" (18). Elsewhere Santiago thinks of the sea "as feminine and as something that gave or withheld great favors, and if she did wild or wicked things it was that she could not help them. The moon affects her as it does a woman, he thought" (30). He consoles himself against his bad luck with "Every day is a new day" (32), and after the marlin jumps on the second night, badly injuring Santiago's right hand, the old fisherman pulls it from the salt water, looks at it, and concludes, "It is not bad. . . . And pain does not matter to a man" (84). In defense of killing the huge Mako shark, Santiago thinks, "everything kills everything else in some way" (106). Finally, in answer to his question of what "beat" him, he declares, "Nothing. . . . I went out too far" (120).

These statements show Santiago's habit of thinking about his experiences in pithy, brief, moralizing sentences, which some readers regard as nuggets of homespun wisdom—little thoughts by which to conduct one's life. They are merely slogans, however—utterances or moralistic tags that sum up experiences superficially.

It means little to say that "a man can be destroyed but not defeated." Rhetoricians can assign meaning to the phrase, but people resort to this kind of clever verbal spin as a moral pick-me-up when things are not going well. To transpose "destroyed" and "defeated" would not affect the meaning of this bromide. Moreover, is pain immaterial to a man? Does the moon affect a woman's behavior? Does everything kill everything else in some way? Did Santiago go out too far?

These questions are rhetorical, of course, because they expect to be answered by "No." Santiago's slogans show his commonplaceness and his mental complacency. They reveal that like many people, he is not genuinely capable of or interested in gaining knowledge of himself or his world. Instead, he takes recourse to banalities that he can impose on his experience: they allow him to avoid having to think about the meaning of his experience. Slogans are like other moralistic or didactic tags: "A stitch in time saves nine," "You can lead a horse to water but you can't make it drink," "A bird in the hand is worth two in the bush." They are quick-fix solutions to complex issues.

These slogans characterize Santiago as an ordinary man of common confusions, a man whose limited intelligence turns to slogans to make meaning out of his world and experience. Nevertheless, his slogans constitute a stylistic problem for the text. If readers do not accept them as appropriate to the ordinary Santiago, then they will likely read them as profound, pompous or pedestrian utterances: if profound, they may portray Santiago as an idealized and exemplary hero of Emersonian dimensions—Man Fishing; if pompous, they may appear to be paternalistic and condescending nuggets paraded for the benefit of those who are morally and intellectually inferior to Santiago; if pedestrian, they may appear so hackneyed that readers feel superior to the author or his narrator or both and dismiss the slogans without considering how they inform the character of Santiago or relate to the novella's issues. Such divergent readings suggest that using slogans puts the narrative at considerable risk and provides evidence for the general critical consensus that the novel is a text fit only for young readers who will not read it critically. For others, however, the slogans have the virtue of challenging readers to justify their function in a text capable of engaging varied responses.

STYLISTIC INEPTNESSES

Regrettably, by the time Hemingway wrote *Old Man* he no longer had the helpful editorial services of either F. Scott Fitzgerald, whose advice improved the final versions of *The Sun Also Rises* and "The Battler," or Maxwell Perkins, the Scribners editor who carefully read Hemingway's work from the mid-1920s until his death in 1947. Hemingway's published fiction was never scrupulously copyedited by his publisher's staff, as some 4,000 errors in *The Sun Also Rises* alone has made evident.[21] Nevertheless, *Old Man* contains several stylistically inept passages that could have profited from a careful editorial eye.

A critical editorial eye would have challenged some of the inappropriate similes, abstractions, and slogans remarked on above, as well as a couple of silly sentences. One occurs when the narrator unnecessarily expresses as fact that Santiago kept his lines "straighter than anyone did" (32). This sounds like a child bragging that he ties his shoe laces neater than anyone else. Another occurs when Santiago, who usually awakened "when he smelled the land breeze," lies asleep in his shack on the eighty-fifth night, the narrator insisting that "tonight the smell of the land breeze came very early and [Santiago] knew it was too early in his dream" (25). Here an editor might have asked whether Hemingway wanted readers to snigger at the idea of an unconscious sleeper consciously knowing the time of night when a smell assailed his nose at the wrong time. Even if intended to characterize Santiago as a strange old man, this sentence stretches the reader's good faith.

Other sentences need help too. On his way up the hill to his shack,

Santiago "stopped for a moment and looked back and saw in the reflection from the street light the great tail of the fish standing up *well* behind the skiff's stern" (121; italics mine). Here the "well" is a squinting modifier, modifying both "standing up" and the preposition "behind." A comma would solve this tiny confusion of whether the erect tail is standing up well or if it is well behind the skiff's stern. Early in the novel when Santiago and Manolin discuss baseball, Manolin comments on Dick Sisler's father, George, whose Hall-of-Fame, 15-year career with the old St. Louis Browns baseball team included two phenomenal seasons: in 1920 he won the batting title with a .407 average; in 1922, with a .420 average, he won both the batting title and the stolen-base title, with 51 steals. But George Sisler was no child star, contrary to Manolin's statement: "The great Sisler's father was never poor and he, the father, was playing in the Big Leagues when he was my age" (22). Born in 1893, George Sisler suited up for the Browns in 1915 at the age of 22, well beyond Manolin's age of 10 to 15 years old.[22] An editorial fact-checker could have cleared up this age discrepancy, for nothing elsewhere in the text suggests that the boy Manolin is into his second decade, and if he is 22 and Santiago has been teaching him to fish for 17 years, then something is quite wrong with Santiago's teaching or Manolin's learning. Such stylistic lapses surely have contributed to the decline in the novella's reputation.

8

Psychology

In his chapter "Nathaniel Hawthorne and 'The Scarlet Letter' " from *Studies in Classic American Literature*, D. H. Lawrence writes,

> All the time there is this split in the American art and art-consciousness. On the top it is as nice as pie, goody-goody and lovey-dovey. Like Hawthorne being such a blue-eyed darling, in life, and Longfellow and the rest such sucking-doves. . . .
>
> Serpents they were. Look at the inner meaning of their art and see what demons they were.
>
> You *must* look through the surface of American art, and see the inner diabolism of the symbolic meaning. Otherwise it is all mere childishness.
>
> That blue-eyed darling Nathaniel knew disagreeable things in his inner soul. He was careful to send them out in disguise.
>
> Always the same. The deliberate consciousness of Americans so fair and smooth-spoken, and the under-consciousness so devilish. *Destroy! destroy! destroy!* hums the under-consciousness. *Love and produce! Love and produce!* cackles the upper-consciousness. And the world hears only the Love-and-produce cackle. Refuses to hear the hum of destruction underneath. Until such time as it will *have* to hear.

> The American has got to destroy. It is his destiny. It is his destiny to destroy the whole corpus of the white psyche, the white consciousness. And he's got to do it secretly.[23]

Although Lawrence directs his observations at nineteenth-century American romantic writers, the destructive underconsciousness that lurks in their work permeates *The Old Man and the Sea* too. Santiago's aggressions—suppress and conceal them though he vainly tries throughout the novella—add the final dimension to his character, for they unlock the psychological enigma and uncanny appeal of his simple-seeming character. The richly ambivalent response of simultaneously attracting and repelling readers is triggered by his overt aggression, his sexism, his passive aggression, his feminization, the harm he inflicts on Manolin, and the pity he deserves from discerning readers. Like all of Hemingway's engaging and problematic heroes, Santiago, too, is a psychological cripple.

SANTIAGO'S OVERT AGGRESSION

Although the novella portrays Santiago as an almost otherworldly figure—a saintly, benevolent, and gentle man—it simultaneously portrays him as very much of this world. One of us, his aggression, fused to his erotic drive, proves his membership in the human race. A number of his aggressions cause little concern. Santiago's acts of aggression against the sharks are of course defensible, because these appetite-driven antagonists instinctually seek to violate his prize. Given his conviction that, as a born fisherman, he must kill the marlin, that act of aggression is occupationally defensible, as is the arm wrestling with the black from Cienfuego, sublimated as it is in a competitive physical contest. Other aggressive actions, however, reveal a cauldron of hostility.

The most flagrant of Santiago's aggressions is the episode that Manolin recalls during the opening conversation of the novella. Santiago asks whether Manolin can remember when, as a five-year-old new to the boat, he was almost killed when Santiago brought in a green fish—one not sufficiently exhausted while being reeled to the boat. The fish came close to tearing the boat to pieces, Manolin recalls, before Santiago could subdue it: "I can remember the tail slapping and banging and the thwart breaking and the noise of the clubbing. I can remember you throwing me into the bow where the wet coiled lines were and feeling the whole boat shiver and the noise of you clubbing him like chopping a tree down and the sweet blood smell all over me" (12). When Santiago asks if Manolin truly remembers the event or just knows it from Santiago's have told it to him, Manolin assures him that he remembers it, for he claims to "remember everything" since they first began fishing together.

This event occurred no more than 10 years earlier, and it seems odd that a skilled fisherman would boat a green fish. His years of experience would have taught him that the fish would battle—vigorously struggle to writhe or flop itself free from the hook and gaff and dodge the lethal clubbing of the fisherman. Perhaps Santiago wanted to display to his new apprentice his strength and skill in boating a big fish quickly. Perhaps Santiago knew there were sharks in the water who would feed off the fish unless he boated it quickly. Perhaps he thought the fish was not hooked firmly and would shake free of the hook if it had enough time. Regardless of his motive, the results of his prompt catch reveal its importance: it allows him to throw Manolin into the bow and to club to death the thwart-breaking, boat-banging, blood-spurting fish.

Manolin's recall of the details of this event testifies to a good memory but better testifies that the event traumatized him. To an impressionable five-year-old child the violence of the episode—the clubbing of the fish, the shivering of the boat, the cracking of the thwart, and the blood-spattering of the activity—would be terrifying. It takes little imagination to visualize Manolin cowering in abject fear in the boat's bow, terror stricken at the sudden emergence of Santiago as a man of murderous potential, a man whose violent behavior could someday, if provoked, turn on him.

Manolin mentions no apology from Santiago for this untoward

episode when it occurred, and during the opening conversation Santiago neither explains why he boated the fish green nor expresses regret at the terrorizing event that occurred. He may have felt no embarrassment over the event and that he had done nothing to apologize for. He may have felt it would not have been manly to apologize for his violent display or his imprudence in having boated the green fish. His failure to express thoughts about his action conflicts with the thoughtfulness and considerateness he shows elsewhere in the novella, however, and also signals to Manolin, perhaps unconsciously, that the old man is capable of committing violence on refractory creatures—including Manolin, should the boy ever choose to struggle against Santiago's domination. Having once witnessed Santiago's capacity for violence, a traumatized or alarmed Manolin would certainly dread a recurrence of such violence and fear that he might be its next victim. That dread contributes to—if not explains—Manolin's submissiveness and deference to Santiago and the absence of self-assertion in him in the novella's opening frame. That absence may be partly due to Manolin's parents' childrearing practices, but it is an absence that Santiago's aggressive action encouraged the boy to adopt.

SANTIAGO'S SEXISM

Except for the killing of the marlin and sharks, the boated green-fish episode is the primary instance of Santiago's overt aggression. This seemingly gratuitous episode occurs in the absence of other thoughts or displays of overt hostility in Santiago, which should lead readers to regard this minimal aggression with suspicion. The absence of overt hostility in Santiago suggests a repressed individual whose fears of overt aggression cause him to find oblique or indirect ways to express it.

One form of such oblique aggression is Santiago's sexism, which expresses hostility or contempt toward things female.[24] The blatant case of Santiago's sexist aggression is his vilification of a jellyfish, the

Portuguese man-of-war. As a man-of-war bird circles above dolphins and flying fish, ineffectually trying to spear one of the latter, Santiago commends "his" efforts and regards "him" "a great help," for "he" leads him to the marlin (33–34), but the old man feels contempt toward the man-of-war jellyfish, which Santiago sees and comments on concurrent with the bird's circlings. He calls it "You whore" (35). To denounce the jellyfish with such a label is inconsistent with Santiago's love-and-fraternity ethic toward creatures animate and objects inanimate. It also is illogical to feminize a creature whose very name—*man-of-war*—assigns it to the opposite gender. Santiago's automatic hatred of the jellyfish, without knowing its actual gender, shows an attitude prejudiced by connections he makes between it and women: when he looks into the water to observe the jellyfish's iridescent bubble, he thinks of it as not only "the falsest thing in the sea" but as a creature whose poisonings "struck like a whiplash" (36). In other words, jellyfish resemble women, both being duplicitous and punitive creatures. Santiago acknowledges his hostility toward this "whore" jellyfish by admitting that he "loved" to see big sea turtles eating them and "loved" to hear jellyfish pop when, after a storm washed them ashore, he could walk the beach and step on them (36). Since the Portuguese man-of-war's gender is never objectively identified, Santiago's gratuitous name calling suggests that jellyfish are scapegoats onto whom he vents misogynistic attitudes that reflect his sexist stereotyping and aggressions.

Santiago's sexism recurs when, during the first night after hooking the marlin, he remarks that the fish "took the bait like a male and he pulls like a male and his fight has no panic in it " (49). Here Santiago discloses his sexist belief that a hooked female marlin always shows "panic." The term, of course, is not descriptive but judgmental. Instead of saying that female marlin fight erratically or feverishly, his term impugns their fight and reveals his belief that under stress they behave in the same way that, he insinuates, women do—with predictable and stereotypical hysteria. The aggression in this putdown, of course, rests in the scorn of "panic"—undesirable behavior, whether of males or females.

Santiago displays no overt aggression toward his wife, whose memory he seems to respect: he has taken down from a wall the tinted photograph of her "because it made him too lonely to see it and it was on the shelf in the corner under his clean shirt" (16). Yet Santiago's failure to think once of his wife during his three-day ordeal suggests repression—some psychic need to erase her from his memory—and that repression suggests that he associates her with unpleasant experiences, either wrongs she committed or guilt for his own actions that he does not want to acknowledge. Either way, his relegation of her photo to a corner shelf beneath a shirt refuses to memorialize her and is tantamount, as all rejections are, to aggressive repudiation of the gender whom she represents in his mind.

These sexist aggressions would appear to be offset by Santiago's love of the sea. As has been discussed earlier the narrator tells that Santiago "always thought of the sea as *la mar* which is what people call her in Spanish when they love her. Sometimes those who love her say bad things of her but they are always said as though she were a woman" (29). Unlike some fishermen who speak of the sea "as *el mar* which is masculine," Santiago "always thought of her as feminine and as something that gave or withheld great favors, and if she did wild or wicked things it was because she could not help them. The moon affects her as it does a woman, he thought" (30).

This litany of sexist aggressions all nests within the metaphoric equation that women and the sea share identical traits. I address his observations in reverse order. First, Santiago denigrates woman–the sea as dependent on the moon or some power over which she has no control. Admittedly the sea is nonvolitional, and its tides and currents are determined by physical laws, but to claim that the same is true of women stereotypes them as dependent and not responsible for their actions, reveals Santiago's stereotyping of woman as puppet. Second, when Santiago thinks of woman–the sea as a creature capable of "wild and wicked things," he further reveals sexist aggression by selecting adjectives of moral disapproval that judge rather than describe behavior. Using nonsexist phrasing, for instance, that passage might have been written, "if she became stormy and gave in to sudden squalls that pounded small vessels." Here, then, Santiago offers another stereotype of woman as evil or treacherous. Third, Santiago cuddles his long-standing notion of woman–the sea "as something that gave or withheld great favors." To be sure, this acknowledges female power, contradicting his earlier characterization of woman–the sea as dependent, but it also insinuates that such power is exercised capriciously or arbitrarily or unpredictably. This is the stereotype of woman as Pandora—an irrational and fickle gift giver.

The fourth and most damning of Santiago's sexist aggressions occurs in the statement that those who love the sea "say bad things of her" but say them "as though she were a woman." With this equation, Santiago indicates that the bad things that people say about the sea are not personal but are only categorical. In this way, the sea becomes a scapegoat for all bad things that men want to say about women. Santiago's unthinking acceptance of unexamined, commonplace attitudes finds nothing wrong in this facile substitution that tolerates any expression of negative feelings or thoughts against women.

Santiago certainly is entitled to his own views on these matters, but he weaves sexist aggressions into the instruction he gives Manolin, thereby perpetuating in another generation his unexamined and slanderous aggressions that demean women. If Santiago is a role model, then these harmful attitudes will surely—and regrettably—be transmitted to his youthful admirers.

SANTIAGO'S PASSIVE AGGRESSION

Despite Santiago's sexist aggressions, many readers find them forgivable when balanced against the love he expresses toward his world. Indeed, his sexist aggressions toward the sea as woman appear negligible when weighed against the love he declares for *la mar* and seem more than offset by the fraternal bond between Manolin and Santiago. Manolin proves that love by patiently waiting at the shore to assist

Santiago on his return from each day's fishing. He helps the old fisherman carry the wooden box with its fishing lines, gaff, and shafted harpoon. He buys Santiago a beer at the Terrace, offers to get sardines and baits for the next day's fishing, and brings him dinner and beer, knowing that Santiago will go hungry before he will beg for a meal or credit from the owner of the Terrace. When Manolin "gently" urges Santiago to eat the dinner the boy has brought to him, Santiago explains his hesitation, saying "I only needed time to wash" (21).

When Santiago mentions that he needed time to wash before he dined, his love for Manolin suddenly is revealed as being tinged with passive aggression. Santiago's comment is expressed nonassertively and without overt reproach but nevertheless is an aggressive barb that triggers guilt and self-accusation in Manolin. The boy scolds himself for not having brought water, soap, and a towel to the hut for Santiago to wash with, which prompts further self-reproach: cold nights and winter are coming, and Manolin has not yet gotten Santiago the shirt, jacket, shoes, and blanket that his old friend will surely need.

Manolin's considerate thoughts and acts are consistent with the text's fraternal theme, but love for Santiago and desire to be his brother's keeper are superficial motives here: Manolin's deeply disturbing motive—guilt—is a result of Santiago's passive aggression. Clearly Manolin has accepted the notion that gratitude is a primary virtue in a young boy. His benevolence toward Santiago, then, partly reflects his attempt to repay Santiago for the instruction and friendship Santiago has shown him. This burden of indebtedness, however, indicates that Manolin knows or senses Santiago's hostility toward him. If Santiago's love was unconflicted Manolin would feel pride in his relationship with Santiago and show signs of pleasure and happiness in his acts of friendship. Instead he feels guilt and shame, ostensibly because his obedience to his father after Santiago's 40 fishless days feels like a betrayal of Santiago, an abandonment of his mentor, an act of filial ingratitude. But Manolin's guilt at having neglected the materials necessary for Santiago's washing before dinner is also symptomatic of the potent insidiousness of Santiago's passive aggression. As a target of

Santiago's indirect and unassertive hostility, Manolin inflicts on himself the punishment he feels that Santiago wishes to administer to him. Manolin's tortured and torturing conscience has been implanted in him by the repressed but nevertheless communicated hostility of Santiago.[25]

At first glance the charge of Santiago's hostility against Manolin may seem irresponsible. Examples of his benevolence, considerateness, and fraternal gentleness toward Manolin occur throughout the novella. Although Santiago has long given Manolin the benefit of his instruction, he will not let him buy him more than two baits or more than one beer at the Terrace. He treats Manolin as an equal. Indeed, he refuses to scold Manolin for neglecting to bring water, soap, and towel to wash up before dinner or, at the end of the novel, to reproach Manolin for failing to declare his discipleship three days earlier. He even gives Manolin the marlin's sword as a trophy and memento of the camaraderie the boy shared with Santiago.

Nevertheless, Santiago's benevolence, considerateness, and fraternal gentleness are excessive and compulsive. Their constant presence, and the marked absence of routine forms of hostility (as when the marlin's lurches injure him), reveal—as do all excessive behaviors—that Santiago successfully arrests the strong temptation and desire to commit aggressive acts and unconsciously fears dread consequences if he releases his aggressive impulses. This behavior seems to constitute what psychologists call *reaction formation*—a defense mechanism of the ego in which individuals actively display excessive and obsessive love or hate toward some activity, object, idea, person or persons, primarily to keep hidden the existence of strong contrary feelings. For instance, an unrelenting and militant antipornography zealot or antiabortion foe might be hiding, in the first case, strong erotic desires to view pornographic scenes or, in the second case, strong aggressive desires to unleash infanticidal longings. Likewise, behind a pornography addict's erotic fixation and active seeking out of pornography may lie strong aggressive attitudes against the subject he or she seems to find only erotic gratification in, and behind militant pro-choice advocates' defense of the rights of women often lies deeper hostility against males whose laws have denied those rights. In any event, individuals whose behavior shows symptoms of passive aggression differ from these examples of people who display reaction formation: the former's excessive and obsessive or compulsive behavior lacks the marked activity of the latter's. Passive aggression, in other words, is a different defense mechanism of the ego, for it shows minimal assertiveness and seeks primarily to deny the existence of aggression. Hiding and vigilantly restraining his aggressive feelings of hostility and malice toward Manolin, Santiago makes them resemble benevolent, altruistic acts whose passivity seems to argue the absence of aggression.

As often occurs in cases of passive aggression, Santiago's passivity triggers aggression in his targets—as it did in Manolin's frenzy over his neglect. Consider Santiago's ordeal with the giant marlin. Santiago is not an aggressor because he only drops his baits into the water and sits in his skiff as the tide, currents, breeze, and oars take him into good water. The marlin, a predator, aggressively eats the bait; Santiago merely sets the hook that the fish bites and swallows. Moreover, the marlin, a powerful fish, tows Santiago to sea; Santiago merely holds the line—the recipient, as it were, of the marlin's aggression. Santiago harpoons the fish only after it is played out, a benevolent coup de grace that puts the fish out of its misery with a quick and merciful death. Throughout the ordeal the fish's aggressions punish Santiago—its lurches injuring his hands and back, cutting his eye, smashing his face into the bow, exhausting the patient fisherman. Santiago seems the victim of the marlin, and his passivity during the ordeal routinely leads readers to esteem his noble behavior and to sympathize with his perseverance.

Readers should note that passive though Santiago's aggression toward the marlin is, it is lethal. It is harmful to Manolin, too, and Santiago's conquest of the fish has its analogue in his conquest of the boy. He desperately desires both conquests, but he conceals one behind his passive aggression by deflecting suspicion as either manipulative or exploitative and by buttressing his altruistic image.

Santiago's passive aggression generates overt aggression in the marlin and similar behavior in Manolin, as the novella's brief scene before Manolin and Santiago's final conversation makes clear. Before Santiago awakens on the last day of the novella, Manolin cries as fishermen gather around Santiago's skiff and fetches a cup of coffee against the time when Santiago will awaken. Manolin's tears register pity for the ordeal he imagines that his mentor has experienced, but they also reflect his own guilt and anger for having failed to pledge himself to Santiago three days earlier. Unlike his scenes in the novella's opening episodes, Manolin how becomes assertive. Expressing himself in imperatives, he orders the proprietor of the Terrace to fix a can of coffee, "Hot and with plenty of milk and sugar in it" (123). Protecting Santiago, first he commands fishermen, "Let no one disturb him" (122), then instructs the Terrace proprietor, "Tell them not to bother Santiago" (123). When the proprietor commends the pair of fine fish Manolin caught on the previous day, the boy retorts, "Damn my fish," dismissing facile condolence and compliment. Manolin's assertive behavior during this prelude to his conversation with Santiago acts out the old fisherman's repressed aggressions, showing how one person's passive aggression stirs active aggression in the person on whom it has been targeted.

Readers often find the closing conversation between Manolin and Santiago a serene coda to a touching relationship between a young boy and an old man, but the conversation also shows the full reach of the duplicitous manipulations in Santiago's passive aggression and warrants detailed examination. When the boy demands that Santiago not sit up and that he drink the coffee Manolin has poured into a glass, Santiago declares, "They beat me, Manolin. . . . They truly beat me" (124). This seems a normal enough opening line for a man who has just survived an ordeal, but the ambiguity of "they" requires Manolin to identify the pronoun's referent, the sharks. Although the pronoun ambiguity can be attributed to the confusion of a just-awakened man, it also is a small act of aggression: its inconsiderateness demands mental labor from Manolin—as ambiguous pronoun referents routinely do (thereby earning retaliatory downgrading from teachers). By saying that the sharks "beat" him, Santiago claims a role as the sharks' victim, altogether minimizing his role as aggressive agent in the killing of the fish. By this inversion of who he is—victim instead of agent—Santiago deliberately downplays his aggression during the ordeal, but thereby reveals his efforts now to conceal the aggression he subtly displays against Manolin. Manolin does not ask him how the sharks beat him but instead vehemently asserts, as the text's italics indicate, that the marlin did not beat Santiago: "*He* didn't beat you. Not the fish" (124). Manolin again takes the aggressive role, for Santiago's incomplete information both compels him to assert what he believes is true and plays on Manolin's guilt at having been absent during the "beating" Santiago got.

More of Santiago's veiled aggression occurs when Manolin asks what Santiago wants done with the marlin's head. He answers, "Let Pedrico chop it up to use in fish traps" (124), permitting another act of aggression—chopping up the fishhead—to be done but not by himself. When Manolin asks what is to be done with the fish's spear, Santiago says, "You keep it if you want it" (124). Because of the size of the fish, Santiago knows that the spear is a valuable trophy. Indeed, the possessor of the marlin's spear will be envied as the inheritor of a prize and esteemed as the beneficiary of everything the spear symbolizes—primarily the legendary status that will be accorded to Santiago as the man who caught the gigantic fish with his bare hands. So the nonchalance in Santiago's conditional answer to Manolin's question— "You keep it *if you want*" (124; italics mine)—is disingenuous. He knows for a certainty that Manolin wants the spear and to pretend otherwise tacitly accuses Manolin of being as indifferent to possessing the spear as he was indifferent to accompanying Santiago three days earlier. In short, Santiago manipulates Manolin by making him declare what Santiago already knows he will say and what would need no saying between strong friends, "I want it" (124).

To sense the full force in the artful aggression of Santiago's "if you want it," consider some lines he could have said without the malicious rebuke couched in that "if" clause: "I'd like you to have it," or "Please take it as a reminder of me," or "I hope you'll want it," or "I'd be honored if you'd keep it as a token of our friendship." Santiago has said and thought sentimental things throughout the text, and a declaration of genuine feeling here would not be inappropriate.

As the conversation proceeds, Santiago continues to rebuke Manolin. After declaring his desire to have the spear, Manolin makes the first of three pledges of discipleship to Santiago, the pledge that Santiago is fishing for with his aggressions: "Now we must make our plans about the other things" (124). If Santiago harbored no aggressive resentment about Manolin's failure to declare his commitment three days earlier, he would promptly acknowledge and appreciate the import of the first-person plural pronouns in Manolin's pledge that "we must make our plans," and he would approve the notion of collaborating on plans for their future. Santiago does no such thing. He brushes aside Manolin's pledge as if it deserved no response or meant little to him. Indeed, Santiago's response—"Did they search for me" (124), does not seem to follow from Manolin's pledge. This non sequitur seems to indicate that Santiago is interested only in what *others* did for him during his absence. It also sets others' actions on his behalf against Manolin's failure to take the necessary step of discipleship three days earlier. In addition, Santiago altogether ignores Manolin's offer to make amends for that failure by resolving to make plans with him for their future. In effect, Santiago insults his offer, as Manolin might conclude, were he later to think over the content of his conversation with Santiago.

Of Santiago's dialogue with Manolin no line contains more passive aggression than his simple declaration, "I missed you" (124). A factual statement, it plainly records the truth: Santiago did miss Manolin during his ordeal, and his several wishes that the boy were with him in the skiff vouch for that fact. But the statement is also an accusation: there would have been no need for Santiago to have missed him if he had decided, albeit against his father's orders, to affiliate himself with Santiago earlier. Nor would Santiago be in a state of physical exhaustion and injury, his statement implies, had he not missed Manolin, for together they might not have been beaten by the sharks and might have gotten home with more of the fish intact. The deep hostility in the simple statement will ring in Manolin's ears after Santiago dies. Given Manolin's devotion to Santiago, this simple statement probably will lead Manolin to accuse himself of bringing on Santiago's death and to remind himself that Santiago would not have been so battered and worn by his lonely ordeal had Manolin been with him. Santiago's simple statement, then, is a harpoon that makes certain that Manolin will feel the thrust of Santiago's charge for years to come. Santiago does nothing to soften the statement—neither admits that it is a selfish idea nor tells Manolin he should not take it personally nor even asks if by chance Manolin missed him as much as he missed Manolin. Any number of qualifications or conditionals could have softened the subtextual severity of Santiago's three words.

Santiago might have allowed Manolin to express how much he too missed Santiago, i 't without a pause—which white space on the page or a newly indented paragraph could express—Santiago promptly asks Manolin what he caught during the three days. This might be another innocent question, were it not for the invidious comparison that Manolin's answer of "four fish" invites. No four fish could begin to rival Santiago's one giant, as he well knows, so his question, which seems asked in genuine interest, has a hostile edge that impugns any fish that Manolin and his fisherman could have caught. The brevity of Manolin's answer reacts to the aggressive barbs in Santiago's question, for he dispenses with it abruptly: "One the first day. One the second and two the third" (124). Manolin admits the insignificance of his fishing in comparison to the ordeal he knows Santiago has been through. So when Santiago commends his catch with "Very good" (125), Manolin's impolite response shows his irritation at Santiago's formal courtesy, blurting out, with manly resolve, "Now we will fish together" (125).

To both this virtual rebuke of Santiago's cold commendation and this second pledge of occupational partnership, Santiago says, with false modesty, "No. I am not lucky. I am not lucky any more" (125).

The passive aggression in this presumably self-effacing statement partly resides in Santiago's self-characterization as one on whom the fates have chosen to turn their backs. This smells of self-pity and also betrays Santiago's resentment toward those forces and agents who have cast him this lot. Rather than overtly retaliate, his statement wheedles aggression from Manolin. The boy assertively declares, "The hell with luck," and boasts with manly swagger, "I'll bring the luck with me" (125). As in his relationship with the marlin, Santiago's passivity again forces the target of his aggressions to be the aggressor.

Having worked Manolin up to this fever pitch of assertive masculinity, Santiago deftly gaffs him with the question to which all of his conversation has led, "What will your family say" (125). As Santiago well knows, before pledging himself to Santiago, Manolin must hurdle the obstacle of disaffiliating himself from his family, a momentous act in the life of a young boy. That Santiago has played his hand well, has employed the talent he earlier boasted of—trickery—is clear with Manolin's retort, "I do not care. I caught two yesterday. But we will fish together now for I still have much to learn" (125). This third pledge from Manolin seems, finally, to satisfy Santiago, whose refusal to accept Manolin's two earlier pledges suggests vindictiveness—a wish to make Manolin pay a penance of one pledge for each day of the ordeal from which he was absent. The aggression that motivates Santiago is clearly evident when he declares, without a moment's hesitation, that the two will need "a good killing lance" (125). It is fitting that Santiago should so readily mention this lethal object, since it is comparable to the verbal aggression he has used on Manolin to subtly coerce his pledge.

To uncover the hostility beneath Santiago's simple-seeming fraternal benevolence requires scrutiny, and to recognize passive aggression in Santiago should help readers be alert to its presence in other people, fictional and real. Victims of passive aggression are duped by its appearance of benevolence or, worse, seduced into imitating it. Consider Twain's Huckleberry Finn or Fitzgerald's Nick Carraway, narrator of *The Great Gatsby*, or Faulkner's Anse Bundren in *As I Lay Dying* or

Steinbeck's George Milton in *Of Mice and Men* or Dickens's title character in *David Copperfield* or Hemingway's Jake Barnes, Thomas Hudson and David Bourne in, respectively, *The Sun Also Rises, Islands in the Stream,* or *Garden of Eden*—to cite just a few examples. These characters appear to be benevolent, passive men and gain reader approval because their lack of aggression makes them vulnerable to others' victimization or exploitation. Yet, to a man, they exploit others and more than a few readers.

Santiago's passive aggression is especially reprehensible because of his choice of victim—an unsuspecting, impressionable boy, easy prey for a man skilled in trickery, on which Santiago prides himself. Following the shrewdly disguised aggressions in the brief conversation between Santiago and Manolin helps expose Santiago's exploitation of a boy to whose naivete must be added the vulnerability of his grief, guilt, and pity for the aged fisherman.

Santiago is not a dyed-in-the-wool villain because he is not fully conscious of his exploitation of Manolin. Although Santiago consciously desires one devotee who will revere him and perpetuate the legend of his name, he does not view this as exploitative. This common confusion, over a parent's, guardian's, teacher's, coach's, guru's, or employer's obligations to the personal rights of subordinates shows that Santiago does not know himself and does not actively seek self-knowledge. He is caught up in the idea of creating someone in his own image, of replicating himself in the young pupil or apprentice. Because he values his own image, he finds no wrong in that replication and would dismiss the idea that it is exploitative. Yet wheedling pledges of discipleship can harm others and has the potential, as well, to precipitate strong guilt feelings and emotional distress in others; it is exploitative because the consent or commitment it coerces from an uninformed or unstable individual is self-serving.

SANTIAGO'S FEMINIZATION

Santiago has strongly ambivalent feelings toward Manolin: he values his friendship and regard but resents his tardiness in pledging discipleship. This tardiness is the overt cause of Santiago's aggressions, but the covert cause is fueled by Santiago's hostility toward his own desire for Manolin. His aggressions reveal his strong disapproval of the latent, unconscious homosexual feelings toward Manolin that he cannot accept in himself. To accept them would require accepting his own lack of masculinity.

Santiago and Manolin's relationship superficially appears to be a heartwarming tale of a fond bonding between young boy and old man. Santiago displays no homosexual overtures or mannerisms. Respecting and respectful of each other, the two seem to share an idealized father-son friendship. Their camaraderie is tainted by the passivity and studied nonsexuality of Santiago's excessive attachment to Manolin, however, which finds him having regressed to an immature stage of development, incapable or undesirous of mature heterosexuality. He prefers the prepubertal sexuality of bonding with a male figure because he fears women as dangerous love objects.

Santiago's behavior replicates the "father fixation" of many young boys, the developmental stage of turning to the father as a way to deflect the anxieties that accompany their forbidden, incestuous, oedipal desire for their mother.[26] Most boys outgrow this stage during puberty and take an active interest in girls, and according to the novella, Santiago did marry a woman who apparently died. Santiago's failure to spend any time with her memory and his recurrent "wish for the boy" constitute a regression to a prepubertal sexual stage that shows his long-standing preference for the passive attachment he can develop toward another male. In this process Santiago, like many another boy, seeks to play what he assumes to be the female role in relation to his father, thereby valuing passivity, seeking approval, and repudiating masculine aims and characteristics. This results in the feminization that characterizes Santiago in the novel. It explains as well Santiago's sexist attitudes, for they reflect—in the indirect way that such unconscious behaviors routinely do—his hostility toward those retained feminine traits in himself that he will neither recognize nor relinquish but will hate. Indeed, his sexist attitudes indicate his resolution to be a "better woman" than most women are, to imitate women and thereby deny both his unconscious hatred of women and the presence of feminine traits in himself. As Karl Menninger writes, "Whenever the development of masculinity is inhibited with a consequent feminine identification, the inhibition is accompanied by a negative attitude toward that femininity within the man himself as well as toward femininity in others." [27] In effect, the battle with the marlin is psychologically vital to the feminized Santiago: it provides him with the ordeal he requires and punishes him for his latent homosexual desire for Manolin's companionship.

All of this feminization adds up to an unhealthy situation for Manolin. The strong bonding that Santiago demands of him is a form of psychological abuse, and Manolin's behavior repeatedly shows that his regard for Santiago rises out of guilt rather than love. If it were love he would feel pride in his activities and take pleasure in the parental approval that Santiago should bestow on him. His guilt shows no pride, however; instead it shows fear of parental rejection, Santiago having infantilized him as an insecure, dependent child. Santiago's latent homosexuality also will lead Manolin away from normal heterosexual development and inculcate the same code of erotic self-denial that Santiago lives by. It will teach Manolin to prefer the intimacy of male over female relationships and to feel guilt should he vary from that model. Finally, Santiago's psychological abuse will foster in Manolin the isolationism that Santiago values and will inflict the conflict that routinely stymies passive aggressives—the conflict between "expressing resentments and wanting to be accepted and admired."[28] In a word, if Santiago's pernicious influence does not make Manolin into a misfit, it will make him into a psychologically disturbed man.

A psychological analysis of Santiago leads me to see Santiago as no ideal figure for Manolin to continue his apprenticeship with. If Santiago's ordeal with the marlin proves to be fatal and he does not survive long then Manolin may have the chance to develop into a healthy young man. He needs to be free from the unhealthy influence of the passive-aggressive cripple with whom he has already fished for too many years.

9

Biographical Matters

Beneath the surface of *The Old Man and the Sea* lie professional anxieties for Ernest Hemingway as his reputation ebbed as a major fiction writer in America and personal anxieties about his public, parental, and filial roles. In 1929 Hemingway's hugely successful *A Farewell to Arms* secured a position that two collections of short stories and *The Sun Also Rises* had promised, but his literary reputation declined in the 1930s, partly because of his nonfiction writing, especially his 1932 bullfighting treatise, *Death in the Afternoon*; his 1935 account of big-game hunting, *Green Hills of Africa*; and the 25 "letters" he wrote for *Esquire* between 1933 and 1936. These letters vaulted him into the public spotlight and made him as famous as any Hollywood celebrity, but literary critics were disdainful. Hemingway tried unsuccessfully to recover his literary stature with the publication of his 1937 novel about a charter-boat fisherman with a social conscience and tragic dimensions, *To Have and Have Not*, but the literary world considered him fading. He tried again with the 1938 collection of previous stories, a Spanish Civil War play, and four recent stories. Excellent though the new stories were, they were not enough to restore him to the highest ranks of American writers.

Finally, the 1940 publication of his Spanish Civil War novel, *For Whom the Bell Tolls*, helped Hemingway regain the status he had held 10 years earlier. This, his most commercially successful book, sold over half a million copies within six months after publication. Even so, in the 1940s his reputation steadily declined, partly because of his wartime activities as correspondent and self-appointed submarine watchdog off the Cuban coast. After the war he could not complete two major novelistic efforts—the posthumously titled *The Garden of Eden* and *Islands in the Stream*. The one novel he did complete, *Across the River and into the Trees* (1950), was a failure, abused by book reviewers and literary critics alike. In the midst of writing the big sea book he completed the draft of *Old Man*, and his publisher and friends urged its publication in the hopes of repudiating the notion that Hemingway no longer had the magic and power his talent had once commanded.

Santiago's perseverence in bringing home his great fish, an act that reestablishes his claim as the community's greatest fisherman, clearly mirrors Hemingway's wish to restore his flagging reputation. With his novella Hemingway regained his status. Even though Hemingway's reputation waned in his final nine years, his 1952 comeback temporarily put to rest his professional anxiety.

The personal anxieties beneath *Old Man* are more complicated, for they deal with his self-image, his relationship to his three sons, and his relationship with his father. All through the 1940s and to the end of his life, Hemingway promoted an image of himself as "Papa." Whether it was with an Italian contessa, movie stars, adulatory writers, or contemporaries, Hemingway liked the name and respect of "Papa." Partly to compensate for his earlier public identity as a macho, hairy-chested womanizer and boastful man of action and appetite, the "Papa" image gratified his need to be regarded as a wise, experienced, avuncular, and benevolent advisor of diminished appetites. This is the image imposed on Santiago, whose fraternal ethic allows "Papa's" paternalism to be expressed. In Hemingway's eyes, Santiago incarnated noble qualities that he saw in his own character. That Hemingway projects himself into such a character, then, reveals an anxiety that he himself is not the man he thinks Santiago is and the wish that he were.

Another source of anxiety stems from Hemingway's neglect of his three sons—John, Patrick and Gregory. Hemingway was never a domestic creature; he fished, took bullfighting trips, covered wars, wrote, fraternized with friends, downed alcoholic beverages, or buried himself in books, newspapers, and correspondence. Except for holiday episodes, the three sons were either traveling between their divorced parents, or away at school, or under the attention, when young, of a nanny. Certainly the sons had great times learning how to fish, ski, hunt, and so forth with their father, and Hemingway was a good father in a medical crisis, as he showed during Patrick's concussion and recovery during the spring of 1947 and during Gregory's emergency appendectomy in June 1949. Despite his domestic self-portrayal in several chapters of his memoir *A Moveable Feast* and in the "Bimini" section of *Islands in the Stream*, however, he was mostly an absentee parent.

This parental neglect appears to have come home to roost during the Christmas holidays of 1950, just before Hemingway began writing *Old Man*. His three sons were no longer under his influence: the eldest, John, was continuing a brief career as a soldier, despite having been an injured prisoner of war near the end of World War II; Patrick was married and ready to leave for Kenya, where he would briefly become a big-game hunting guide; the youngest, Gregory, was a bold, rebellious, and bright 19-year-old who challenged his father's parental and marital conduct. As Hemingway experienced anxiety over his loss of influence over these three departing or defecting sons, Santiago wishes "that the boy were here," regrets that he is without his "son," and expresses hurt that his "son" has abandoned him for another fisherman.

Hemingway's anxiety that he failed to secure his sons' regard and respect, then, may explain why Santiago perseveres with the marlin and commits himself to going "out too far" to capture it. Both behaviors externalize Hemingway's wishes—first, to make amends for his failure to maintain a continuous relationship with his sons, and, second, to make commitments that far exceeded those of any other parent if they were required to regain his influence over any of his sons. Further evidence of Hemingway's preoccupation with his parental neglect lies in the novel in which *Old Man* was originally embedded, *Islands in the Stream*. In that novel a father loses two sons in an automobile accident and a third son in the war, objectifying Hemingway's private anxiety.

Finally, the deepest level of personal anxiety reflected in the novella is Hemingway's relationship to his father. When Dr. Clarence "Ed" Hemingway took his life in early December 1928, Hemingway found two scapegoats on whom he could blame his father's "cowardly act," as Hemingway regarded it—an uncle who refused to help the doctor out of some financial worries and Hemingway's overbearing mother, against whom he bore a lifelong grudge and hostility, although she shared many of his own qualities. All his remaining life Hemingway brooded over his father's suicide, knowing nothing of the hemachro-matosis that genetically may have brought about his own eventual suicide as well as the suicides of his brother and probably two of his sisters.[29] And Hemingway's brooding led him to see himself as an accomplice in his father's suicide and led him to distance himself from the father toward whom he had always been strongly ambivalent. His published work found scant favor in the eyes of his father, who felt that it was a betrayal of the values he had tried so hard to instill in his son. Hemingway may never have seen himself as his father did—as a son who betrayed and abandoned him—but at the deepest level of *The Old Man and the Sea* may lie Hemingway's apology, his Manolin-like remorse at having failed to stand by his father and see him through his difficult final years. In the battered and exhausted Santiago whom Manolin nurses at the novella's end, Hemingway may have seen the father who suffered through one too many ordeals with physical infir-mities, financial shortfalls, and domestic disharmonies. The novella may well be Hemingway's belated apology for not having recognized his father's need for him—for having been deaf to his father's distant whisperings of "I wish the boy were here."

Epilogue

One of my favorite passages in Hemingway's work begins chapter 14 of *Death in the Afternoon*:

> The bullfighter's ideal, what he hopes will always come out of the toril and into the ring is a bull that will charge perfectly straight and will turn by himself at the end of each charge and charge again perfectly straight and will turn by himself at the end of each charge and charge again perfectly straight; a bull that charges as straight as though he were on rails. He hopes for him always, but such a bull will come, perhaps, only once in thirty or forty. The bullfighters call them round-trip bulls, go-and-come bulls, cariles, or mounted-on-rails bulls, and those bullfighters who have never learned to dominate difficult bulls nor how to correct their faults, simply defend themselves against the regular run of animals and wait for one of these straight charging bulls to attempt any brilliant work. These bullfighters are the ones who have never learned to fight bulls, who have skipped their apprenticeship by being promoted to matadors because of some great afternoon in Madrid, or a series in the provinces, with bulls that charged to suit them. They have art, personalities, when the personalities are not scared out of them, but no *metier* and, since

courage comes with confidence, they are often frightened simply because they do not know their trade properly. They are not naturally cowardly or they would never have become bullfighters, but they are made cowardly by having to face difficult bulls without the knowledge, experience or training to handle them, and since out of ten bulls that they fight there may not be a one that will be the ideal animal that they only know how to work with, most of the times you will see them their work will be dull, defensive, ignorant, cowardly and unsatisfactory. If you see them with the animal that they want you will think that they are wonderful, exquisite, brave, artistic and sometimes almost unbelievable in the quietness and closeness with which they will work to the bull. But if you see them day in and day out unable to give a competent performance with any bull that offers any difficulty whatsoever you will wish for the old days of competently trained fighters and to hell with phenomenons and artists.[30]

This passage may seem to be about something altogether foreign to *The Old Man and the Sea*, but Hemingway's discussion of bullfighters and the kind of bulls they wish will enter the bull ring is analogous to the experience readers have when a book enters the arena of their lives. Many readers are like Hemingway's ill-trained or poorly experienced bullfighters—unable to grapple with a difficult book, ill at ease with its failure to be a "mounted-on-rails" book, uncomfortable with issues that do not charge straight, turn, and then charge straight again. Readers may fault the book and not themselves as readers who need better training and more experience.

Many readers fault *Old Man* as a "mounted-on-rails" book over which they can demonstrate their superiority. Given the novella's reputation as a simple test undeserving of the attention reserved for masterpieces, it may well deserve that "mounted-on-rails" status. The text is deeply problematic, however, inasmuch as it leads to the sharply divergent readings that have been explored in this study. The text surely is no "mounted-on-rails" novella: it leads readers to ask questions, weigh problems, and discuss disputes. It provokes readers to debate the many issues examined in this book. A "mounted-on-rails" text does not do that; a masterwork does.

Notes and References

1. The following works have been consulted for this chapter: Paul Boyer, *By the Bomb's Early Light: American Thought and Culture at the Dawn of the Atomic Age* (New York: Pantheon, 1985); Paul A. Carter, *Another Part of the Fifties* (New York: Columbia University Press, 1983); Herbert Druks, *From Truman through Johnson: A Documentary History*, vol. 1 (New York: Robert Speller & Sons, 1971); Eric F. Goldman *The Crucial Decade—and After: America, 1945–60* (New York: Random House, 1960); J. Ronald Oakley, *God's Country: America in the Fifties* (New York: Dembner Books, 1986); William L. O'Neill, ed., introduction to *American Society since 1945* (Chicago: Quadrangle Books, 1969); Joseph Satin, ed., *The 1950s: America's "Placid" Decade* (Boston: Houghton Mifflin, 1960); I. F. Stone, *The Haunted Fifties* (New York: Random House, 1963).

2. "An American Storyteller," *Time*, 13 December 1954, 72.

3. *Ernest Hemingway: Selected Letters, 1917–1961,* ed. Carlos Baker (New York: Charles Scribner's Sons, 1981), 738.

4. Edward Weeks, "Hemingway at His Best," *Atlantic*, September 1952, 72; Harvey Breit, "Hemingway's *Old Man*," *Nation*, 6 September 1952, 194; Robert Gorham Davis, "The Story of a Tragic Fisherman," *New York Times Book Review*, 7 September 1952, 1; Fanny Butcher, "Hemingway at His Incomparable Best: New Novella Ranked with *Moby-Dick*," *Chicago Sunday Tribune*, 7 September 1952, 3; Joseph Henry Jackson, "Hemingway at His Best in a Story of a Fisherman and His Catch," *San Francisco Chronicle*, 7 September 1952, 22; Henry Seidel Canby, "An Unforgettable Picture of Man against the Sea and Man against Fate," *Book-of-the-Month Club News*, August 1952, 2; William Faulkner, *Shenandoah* (Autumn 1952): 55.

5. Orville Prescott, "Books of the Times," *New York Times*, 28 August 1952, 21; R. W. B. Lewis, "Eccentrics' Pilgrimage," *Hudson Review* (Spring 1953): 147; Mark Schorer, "With Grace under Pressure," *New Republic*, 6 October 1952, 19; Delmore Schwartz, "Long after Eden," *Partisan Review* (November–December 1952): 702.

6. Seymour Krim, "Ernest Hemingway: Valor and Defeat," *Commonweal,* 19 September 1952, 584–86; Philip Rahv, "Latest Hemingway and Steinbeck," *Commentary* (October 1952): 390–91; John W. Aldridge, "About Ernest Hemingway," *Virginia Quarterly Review* (Spring 1953): 312–13; Milton Howard, "Hemingway and Heroism," *Masses and Mainstream,* October 1952, 1–8.

7. Philip Young, *Ernest Hemingway* (New York: Rinehart, 1952), 100, 113; Leo Gurko, "The Old Man and the Sea," *College English* 17 (October 1955): 14; Clinton S. Burhans, Jr., "*The Old Man and the Sea*: Hemingway's Tragic Vision of Man," *American Literature* 31 (January 1960): 447.

8. Carlos Baker, "The Ancient Mariner," in his *Hemingway: The Writer as Artist* (Princeton, N.J.: Princeton University Press, 1956), 289–328; Joseph Waldmeir, "Confiteor Hominem: Ernest Hemingway's Religion of Man," *Papers of the Michigan Academy of Science, Arts, and Letters* 42 (1957): 349–56; Arvin S. Wells, "A Ritual of Transfiguration: *The Old Man and the Sea,*" *University Review* 30 (Winter 1963): 97.

9. Earl Rovit, *Ernest Hemingway* (Boston: Twayne, 1963), 88–90; Bickford Sylvester, "Hemingway's Extended Vision: *The Old Man and the Sea,*" *PMLA* 81 (March 1966): 132, 135, 136.

10. Wirt Williams, *The Tragic Art of Ernest Hemingway* (Baton Rouge: Louisiana State University Press, 1981), 172–97; Philip Toynbee, "Hemingway," *Encounter,* October 1961, 87; Robert P. Weeks, "Fakery in *The Old Man and the Sea,*" *College English* 24 (December 1962): 188–92; Philip Young, *Ernest Hemingway: A Reconsideration* (University Park: Pennsylvania State University Press, 1966), 274.

11. Wolfgang Wittkowski, "Crucified in the Ring: Hemingway's *The Old Man and the Sea*" (1967), trans. Bonita Veysey and Larry Wells, *Hemingway Review* 3 (Fall 1983): 4; Claire Rosenfield, "New World, Old Myths," in *Twentieth Century Interpretations of "The Old Man and the Sea": A Collection of Critical Essays,* ed. Katharine T. Jobes (Englewood Cliffs, N.J.: Prentice-Hall, 1968), 51; Jackson J. Benson, *Hemingway . . . The Writer's Art of Self-Defense* (Minneapolis: University of Minnesota Press, 1969), 171, 172, 180.

12. Kenneth G. Johnston, "The Star in Hemingway's *The Old Man and the Sea,*" *American Literature* 42 (1970): 388–91; Joseph H. Flora, "Biblical Allusions in *The Old Man and the Sea,*" *Studies in Short Fiction* 10 (1973): 143–47; George Monteiro, "Santiago, DiMaggio, and Hemingway: The Ageing Professionals of *The Old Man and the Sea,*" in *Fitzgerald/Hemingway Annual 1975,* ed. Matthew J. Bruccoli and C. E. Frazer Clark, Jr. (Englewood, Colo.: Information Handling Services, 1975), 273–80; Linda Wagner, "The Poem of Santiago and Manolin," *Modern Fiction Studies* 19 (1973–74): 517–29; Sam S. Baskett, "The Great Santiago: Opium, Vocation, and Dream in *The*

Notes and References

Old Man and the Sea," in *Fitzgerald/Hemingway Annual 1976*, ed. Matthew J. Bruccoli (Englewood, Colo.: Information Handling Services, 1976), 230–42.

13. Ben Stoltzfus, *Gide and Hemingway: Rebels against God* (Port Washington, N.Y.: Kennikat Press, 1978), 43, 44, 47; Gerry Brenner *Concealments in Hemingway's Works* (Columbus: Ohio State University Press, 1983), 177–87.

14. Martin Swan, *"The Old Man and the Sea*: Women Taken for Granted,"* in *Visages de la féminité*, ed. A.-J. Bullier and J.-M. Racault (St. Denis, France: Université de Réunion, 1984), 147–63; Ben Stoltzfus, *"The Old Man and the Sea*: A Lacanian Reading,"* in *Hemingway: Essays of Reassessment*, ed. Frank Scafella (New York: Oxford University Press, 1991), 190–99.

15. Kenneth Lynn, *Hemingway* (New York: Simon & Schuster, 1987), 566. On p. 563 Lynn cites Gregory Hemingway's irreverent judgment.

16. *By-Line: Ernest Hemingway, Selected Articles and Dispatches of Four Decades*, ed. William White (New York: Charles Scribner's Sons, 1967), 239–40.

17. Norberto Fuentes, *Hemingway in Cuba*, trans. Consuelo E. Corwin, ed. Larry Alson (Secaucus, N.J.: Lyle Stuart, 1984), 241–42.

18. Joseph Conrad, *Lord Jim* (1899; New York: Washington Square Press, 1963), 68.

19. Robert Scholes, "Toward a Semiotics of Literature," in his *Semiotics and Interpretation* (New Haven, Conn.: Yale University Press, 1982), 17–36.

20. Samuel E. Longmire, "Hemingway's Praise of Dick Sisler in *The Old Man and the Sea*," *American Literature* 42 (1970): 96–98.

21. James Hinkle, " 'Dear Mr. Scribner'—about the Published Text of *The Sun Also Rises*," *Hemingway Review* 6, no. 1 (1986): 43–64.

22. For an ingenious explanation of how Manolin's statement reveals him to be no more than 10, see C. Harold Hurley, "Just 'a Boy,' or 'Already a Man?': Manolin's Age in *The Old Man and the Sea*," *Hemingway Review* 10, no. 2 (1991): 71–72.

23. D. H. Lawrence, *Studies in Classic American Literature* (1923; New York: Viking Press, 1964), 83–84.

24. For a different analysis of the novella's sexist attitudes, see Martin Swan, *"The Old Man and the Sea*: Women Taken for Granted," 147–63.

25. A good deal of debate surrounds the label of passive aggression—whether it is a specific personality disorder, a defense mechanism, or a maladaptive personality trait. As will be clear from my discussion, I use it to mean a defense mechanism of the ego. For discussion of the term and its varied uses, see Joseph T. McCann, "Passive-Aggressive Personality Disorder: A Review," *Journal of Personality Disorders* 2 (1988):170–79.

26. My discussion here and in the following discussion is indebted to Karl Menninger's classic, *Love against Hate* (New York: Harcourt, Brace & World, 1942), especially the chapter "The Frustrations of Women," 41–79.

27. Menninger, 58.

28. McCann, 172.

29. Susan F. Beegel, "Hemingway and Hemochromatosis," *Hemingway Review* 10, no. 1 (1990): 57–66.

30. *Death in the Afternoon* (New York: Charles Scribner's Sons, 1932), 160–61.

Selected Bibliography

Primary Works

Novels

The Torrents of Spring. New York: Charles Scribner's Sons, 1926.

The Sun Also Rises. New York: Charles Scribner's Sons, 1926.

A Farewell to Arms. New York: Charles Scribner's Sons, 1929.

To Have and Have Not. New York: Charles Scribner's Sons, 1937.

For Whom the Bells Tolls. New York: Charles Scribner's Sons, 1940.

Across the River and into the Trees. New York: Charles Scribner's Sons, 1950.

The Old Man and the Sea. New York: Charles Scribner's Sons, 1952.

Islands in the Stream. [Edited by Mary Hemingway and Charles Scribner, Jr.] New York: Charles Scribner's Sons, 1970.

The Garden of Eden. [Edited by Tom Jenks.] New York: Charles Scribner's Sons, 1986.

Short Story Collections

In Our Time. New York: Boni & Liveright, 1925.

Men without Women. New York: Charles Scribner's Sons, 1927.

Winner Take Nothing. New York: Charles Scribner's Sons, 1933.

The Fifth Column and the First Forty-nine Stories. New York: Charles Scribner's Sons, 1938.

The Fifth Column and Four Stories of the Spanish Civil War. New York: Charles Scribner's Sons, 1969.

The Nick Adams Stories. [Edited by Philip Young.] New York: Charles Scribner's Sons, 1972.

The Complete Short Stories of Ernest Hemingway. [Edited by Charles Scribner, Jr.] New York: Charles Scribner's Sons, 1987.

Nonfiction

Death in the Afternoon. New York: Charles Scribner's Sons, 1932.

Green Hills of Africa. New York: Charles Scribner's Sons, 1935.

A Moveable Feast. [Edited by Mary Hemingway and L. H. Brague, Jr.] New York: Charles Scribner's Sons, 1964.

By-Line: Ernest Hemingway, Selected Articles and Dispatches of Four Decades. Edited by William White. New York: Charles Scribner's Sons, 1967.

Ernest Hemingway: Selected Letters, 1917–1961. Edited by Carlos Baker. New York: Charles Scribner's Sons, 1981.

The Dangerous Summer. [Edited by Charles Scribner, Jr., and Michael Pietsch.] New York: Charles Scribner's Sons, 1985.

Ernest Hemingway: Dateline Toronto: The Complete Toronto Star Dispatches, 1920–1924. Edited by William White. New York: Charles Scribner's Sons, 1985.

Secondary Works

Bibliographies and Reference Works

August, Jo. *Catalog of the Ernest Hemingway Collection at the John F. Kennedy Library.* 2 vols. Boston: G. K. Hall, 1982. Unindexed, descriptive listing of documents accessible to researchers as of 1982.

Brasch, James D., and Joseph Sigman. *Hemingway's Library: A Composite Record.* New York: Garland, 1981. Well-indexed, comprehensive listing of the 7,700 books in Hemingway's various libraries.

DeFazio, Albert J. "Hemingway Bibliography." In *Hemingway Review.* Ada: Ohio Northern University, 1988–.

Hanneman, Audre. *Ernest Hemingway: A Comprehensive Bibliography.* Princeton: Princeton University Press, 1967. Meticulously described and

Selected Bibliography

scrupulously cross-referenced compilation of work by and on Hemingway; includes excerpts and hard-to-use index.

————. *Supplement to Ernest Hemingway: A Comprehensive Bibliography*. Princeton: Princeton University Press, 1975. Adds overlooked and new entries between 1966 and 1973.

White, William. "Hemingway Checklist." In *Fitzgerald/Hemingway Annual 1969–1979*. Washington, D.C.: NCR Microcard Editions, 1969–74. Englewood, Colo.: Information Handling Services, 1975–76. Detroit: Gale Research, 1977–80.

————. "Current Bibliography." In *Hemingway Notes*. Ada: Ohio Northern University, 1979–81.

————. "Current Bibliography." In *Hemingway Review*. Ada: Ohio Northern University, 1981–87.

Biographies and Memoirs

Baker, Carlos. *Ernest Hemingway: A Life Story*. New York: Charles Scribner's Sons, 1969. Detailed, well-documented, and discreet "authorized" biography.

Castillo-Puche, Jose Luis. *Hemingway in Spain: A Personal Reminiscence of Hemingway's Years in Spain by His Friend*. Translated by Helen R. Lane. Garden City, N.Y.: Doubleday, 1974. Impressionistic reminiscences of a psychologically troubled Hemingway between 1954 and 1960.

Fuentes, Norberto. *Hemingway in Cuba*. Translated by Consuelo E. Corwin. Edited by Larry Alson. Secaucus, N.J.: Lyle Stuart, 1984. Baggy but engaging account of Hemingway's 22 years in Cuba.

Hemingway, Gregory H. *Papa: A Personal Memoir*. Boston: Houghton Mifflin, 1976. Youngest son's guilt-ridden memoir of times with "Papa."

Hemingway, Mary Welsh. *How It Was*. New York: Knopf, 1976. Fourth wife's diary-driven account of life with Hemingway, 1944–1961.

Hotchner, A. E. *Papa Hemingway: A Personal Memoir*. New York: Random House, 1966. Reprinted with provocative postscript and new subtitle, "The Ecstasy and Sorrow." New York: William Morrow, 1983. Anecdotal memoir of Hemingway's last 14 years.

Lynn, Kenneth. *Hemingway*. New York: Simon & Schuster, 1987. Psychoanalytically provocative and historically grounded biography, emphasizing Hemingway's fixation on his mother.

Meyers, Jeffrey. *Hemingway: A Biography*. New York: Harper & Row, 1985.

Irreverent and illuminating account, drawing on archival materials, interviews, FBI files, and Hemingway's medical history.

Reynolds, Michael. *The Young Hemingway*. New York: Basil Blackwell, 1986. *Hemingway: The Paris Years*. Cambridge, Mass.: Basil Blackwell, 1989. Detailed accounts of Hemingway's early decades in projected four- or five-volume "definitive" biography.

Sanford, Marcelline Hemingway. *At the Hemingways: A Family Portrait*. Boston: Atlantic–Little, Brown, 1962. Older sister's anecdotal version of growing up in the Hemingway households.

Critical Studies: Books

Baker, Carlos. *Hemingway: The Writer as Artist*. 4th ed. Princeton: Princeton University Press, 1972. Biographically saturated, symbol-driven, and reverential analysis of the works through *Islands in the Stream*; the first book for serious Hemingway students.

Baker, Sheridan. *Ernest Hemingway: An Introduction and Interpretation*. New York: Holt, Rinehart & Winston, 1967. Brief, balanced, and well-written reading of work through *Old Man*.

Benson, Jackson J. *Hemingway . . . The Writer's Art of Self-Defense*. Minneapolis: University of Minnesota Press, 1969. Varied reading of Hemingway's experimentation and exorcism of emotional problems through art.

Brenner, Gerry. *Concealments in Hemingway's Works*. Columbus: Ohio State University Press, 1983. Psychoanalytic, chronological, and revisionist reading of Hemingway's experiments, concealed esthetic, and father fixation.

Grebstein, Sheldon Norman. *Hemingway's Craft*. Carbondale: Southern Illinois University Press, 1973. Analysis of Hemingway's craftsmanship: fictional structures, sophisticated narration, dialogue, and style.

Gurko, Leo. *Ernest Hemingway and the Pursuit of Heroism*. New York: Thomas Y. Crowell, 1968. Simplistic and morally certain reading of the anguished searches of Hemingway's heroes.

Hovey, Richard B. *Hemingway: The Inward Terrain*. Seattle: University of Washington Press, 1968. Mildly Freudian analysis of work through *A Moveable Feast*.

Killinger, John. *Hemingway and the Dead Gods: A Study in Existentialism*. Lexington: University of Kentucky Press, 1960. Provocative monograph of links between Hemingway's crisis-oriented individualists and existentialist thought.

Selected Bibliography

Laurence, Frank M. *Hemingway and the Movies*. Jackson: University Press of Mississippi, 1981. Detailed comparison of Hemingway's fictions with their film versions, but lacking good film bibliography.

Lewis, Robert W., Jr. *Hemingway on Love*. Austin: University of Texas Press, 1965. Developmental charting of Hemingway's heroes from selfish to selfless love.

Peterson, Richard K. *Hemingway: Direct and Oblique*. The Hague and Paris: Mouton, 1969. Close examination of Hemingway's styles and perceptive questioning of his techniques, purposes, and effectiveness.

Rovit, Earl. *Ernest Hemingway*. Boston: Twayne, 1963. Revised edition with Gerry Brenner. Boston: G. K. Hall, 1986. Useful, eclectic, and well-written discussion of Hemingway's work through *The Dangerous Summer*.

Stephens, Robert O. *Hemingway's Nonfiction: The Public Voice*. Chapel Hill: University of North Carolina Press, 1968. Methodical discussion, documentation, and categorization of Hemingway's exposition.

Stoltzfus, Ben. *Gide and Hemingway: Rebels against God*. Port Washington, N.Y.: Kennikat Press, 1978. Revisionist reading of *Old Man's* religious allusions.

Waldhorn, Arthur. *A Reader's Guide to Ernest Hemingway*. New York: Farrar, Straus & Giroux, 1972. Succinct, well-written overview of Hemingway and his works.

Williams, Wirt. *The Tragic Art of Ernest Hemingway*. Baton Rouge: Louisiana State University Press, 1981. Developmental analysis of the parallel between Hemingway's fiction and his tragic vision, which culminates in *Old Man*.

Wylder, Delbert. *Hemingway's Heroes*. Albuquerque: University of New Mexico Press, 1969. Perceptive differentiation among the heroes through *Old Man*, seeing Santiago as "saintly, but sinfully human as well."

Young, Philip. *Ernest Hemingway*. New York: Rinehart, 1952. Revised as *Ernest Hemingway: A Reconsideration*. University Park: Pennsylvania State University Press, 1966. Tracing and articulation of the "wound theory" in Hemingway's works; the second book for students to examine.

Critical Studies: Collections

Baker, Carlos, ed. *Hemingway and His Critics: An International Anthology*. New York: Hill & Wang, 1961. Twenty essays, three-fourths written in the 1950s, one-third by international critics.

Jobes, Katharine T., ed. *Twentieth Century Interpretations of "The Old Man and the Sea": A Collection of Critical Essays.* Englewood Cliffs, N.J.: Prentice-Hall, 1968. Nine long and nine short essays or excerpts, showing sharply divergent interpretations and opinions of the novella's worth.

McCaffery, John K. M., ed. *Ernest Hemingway: The Man and His Work.* Cleveland: World Publishing, 1950. Twenty-one reviews, magazine articles, journal essays, and chapters from books, all written in the 1930s and 1940s.

Meyers, Jeffrey, ed. *Hemingway: The Critical Heritage.* Boston: Routledge & Kegan Paul, 1982. Four obituaries and 118 magazine essays and book reviews, three-fourths by Americans.

Stephens, Robert O., ed. *Ernest Hemingway: The Critical Reception.* New York: Burt Franklin, 1977. Nearly 400 newspaper and magazine reviews of books through *The Nick Adams Stories,* sometimes in their entirety, often excerpted, occasionally paraphrased.

Wagner, Linda Welshimer, ed. *Ernest Hemingway: Five Decades of Criticism.* East Lansing: Michigan State University Press, 1974. Twenty essays, six from the 1950s, 13 from the 1960s, one from 1924.

———. *Ernest Hemingway: Six Decades of Criticism.* East Lansing: Michigan State University Press, 1987. Twenty-eight essays, none from the 1974 collection above, three previously unpublished, 13 from the 1980s, six from the 1970s, and two or three from the previous decades.

Weeks, Robert P., ed. *Hemingway: A Collection of Critical Essays.* Englewood Cliffs, N.J.: Prentice-Hall, 1962. Sixteen excerpts and essays that, despite the publication date, make this still the most provocative of the critical anthologies.

Critical Studies: Articles

Baskett, Sam S. "Toward a 'Fifth Dimension' in *The Old Man and the Sea.*" *Centennial Review* 19 (Summer 1975):269–86. Pairing of arcane Christian analogues and motifs of "strangeness" that suggest mystery and " 'another intensity' in which the old man moves," carrying "Santiago's experience beyond 'the captive now.' "

———. "The Great Santiago: Opium, Vocation, and Dream in *The Old Man and the Sea.*" In *Fitzgerald/Hemingway Annual 1976,* edited by Matthew J. Bruccoli, 230–42. Englewood, Colo.: Information Handling Services, 1978. Detailed analysis of baseball allusions to argue that the recurrent use of "great" refers to Santiago, not to Joe DiMaggio.

Burhans, Clinton, S. Jr. "*The Old Man and the Sea*: Hemingway's Tragic Vision of Man." *American Literature* 31 (January 1960):446–55. Reprinted in *Hemingway and His Critics*, edited by Carlos Baker, 259–68, and in *Twentieth Century Interpretations of "The Old Man and the Sea,"* edited by Katharine T. Jobes, 72–80. Reverential reading of the theme of interdependency between saintly Santiago and the creatures and elements of his universe.

Byrne, Janice F. "New Acquisitions Shed Light on *The Old Man and the Sea* Sources." *Hemingway Review* 10 (Spring 1991):68–70. Examination of a notebook and a carbon copy of the log of Hemingway's fishing boat *Pilar* for kernels of Santiago's story as early as 1932 or 1933.

Cooperman, Stanley. "Hemingway and Old Age: Santiago as Priest of Time." *College English* 27 (December 1965):388–91. Humanistic reading of novella as "a poem of reconciliation to the meaning and nature of age itself," "a hymn of praise to the sacred nature of action when purified by will and uncorrupted by external cause."

Dittmar, Linda. "Larding the Text: Problems in Filming *The Old Man and the Sea*." In *A Moving Picture Feast: The Filmgoer's Hemingway*, edited by Charles M. Oliver, 54–63. New York: Praeger, 1989. Detailed analysis of difficulties in John Sturges's filmic adaptation.

Flora, Joseph H. "Biblical Allusions in *The Old Man and the Sea*." *Studies in Short Fiction* 10 (1973):143–47. Anagogical discussion of Santiago as ironic counterpoint to Simon Peter, whom Jesus exhorted to "Launch out into the deep" (Luke 5:4).

Hamilton, John Bowen. "Hemingway and the Christian Paradox." *Renascence* 24 (Spring 1972):141–54. Examination of the novella's emphasis on the symbolic meanings of the fish, *Ichthus*, as acronym for Christ.

Heaton, C. P. "Style in *The Old Man and the Sea*." *Style* 4 (1970):11–27. Exhaustive analysis of sentence types, word-length and -choice, punctuation, figures of speech, and ratios of dialogue to exposition.

Hofling, Dr. Charles K. "Hemingway's *The Old Man and the Sea* and the Male Reader." *American Imago* 20 (Summer 1963):161–73. Psychoanalytic reading of Santiago's unambivalent behavior toward Manolin and the reader's identification with Santiago's regressive, adolescent-stage experience.

Hurley, C. Harold. "Just 'a Boy' or 'Already a Man?': Manolin's Age in *The Old Man and the Sea*." *Hemingway Review* 10 (Spring 1991):71–72. Interpretation claiming Hemingway knew that Manolin's ambiguous statement about the Sislers "held the key to Manolin's age"—no older than 10, Dick Sisler's age when his father George retired from baseball in 1930.

Johnston, Kenneth G. "The Star in Hemingway's *The Old Man and the Sea*." *American Literature* 42 (1970):388–91. Analysis of the constellation Orion the Hunter and the relevance of Rigel—"the brilliant white star embedded in Orion's left foot"—to the novella's foot motif.

Longmire, Samuel E. "Hemingway's Praise of Dick Sisler in *The Old Man and the Sea*." *American Literature* 42 (1970):96–98. Explanation of Sisler's Cuban fame for hitting four home runs in two days, one a giant.

Mansell, Darrel. "When Did Ernest Hemingway Write *The Old Man and the Sea?*" In *Fitzgerald/Hemingway Annual 1975*, edited by Matthew J. Bruccoli, and C. E. Frazer Clark, Jr., 311–24. Englewood, Colo.: Information Handling Services, 1975. Well-researched and cautious conjecture that Hemingway wrote the novella in 1935–36.

Monteiro, George. "Santiago, DiMaggio, and Hemingway: The Ageing Professionals of *The Old Man and the Sea*." In *Fitzgerald/Hemingway Annual 1975*, edited by Matthew J. Bruccoli and C. E. Frazer Clark, Jr., 273–80. Englewood, Colo.: Information Handling Services, 1975. Retrieval of journalistic accounts of DiMaggio's recovery and performance after heel surgery to compare Santiago's ordeal against his.

Prizel, Yuri. "The Critics and *The Old Man and the Sea*." *Research Studies* 41 (1973):208–16. Review of criticism on the novella.

Rosenfield, Claire. "New World, Old Myths." In *Twentieth Century Interpretations of "The Old Man and the Sea*," edited by Katharine T. Jobes, 41–55. Examination of mythic analogues in *Old Man* and Faulkner's "The Bear."

Stoltzfus, Ben. "*The Old Man and the Sea*: A Lacanian Reading." In *Hemingway: Essays of Reassessment*, edited by Frank Scafella, 190–99. New York: Oxford University Press, 1991. Semiotic examination of central words that reveal Santiago's unconscious desires.

Swan, Martin. "*The Old Man and the Sea*: Women Taken for Granted." In *Visages de la féminité*, edited by A.-J. Bullier and J.-M. Racault, 147–63. St. Denis, France: Université de Réunion, 1984. Feminist analysis of Hemingway's hostility toward the novella's female characters and entities.

Sylvester, Bickford. "Hemingway's Extended Vision: *The Old Man and the Sea*." *PMLA* 81 (March 1966):130–38. Reprinted in *Twentieth Century Interpretations of "The Old Man and the Sea,"* edited by Katharine T. Jobes, 81–96. Reexamination of the man-nature relationship in the novella, arguing the paradoxical fusion of affection and violence in Santiago's actions.

Wagner, Linda W. "The Poem of Santiago and Manolin." *Modern Fiction Studies* 19 (1973–74):517–29. Reprinted in her *Ernest Hemingway: Six Decades of Criticism*, 275–87. Comparison of relationship between Thomas and David Hudson of *Islands in the Stream* and Santiago and Manolin to show the depth of selfless love in the latter pair.

Selected Bibliography

Waldmeir, Joseph. "Confiteor Hominem: Ernest Hemingway's Religion of Man." *Papers of the Michigan Academy of Sciences, Arts, and Letters* 42 (1957):349–56. Reprinted in *Hemingway: A Collection of Critical Essays,* edited by Robert P. Weeks, 161–68. Loosely allegorical reading of Christian symbols and abstractions to argue Hemingway's secularized religion of Manhood.

Weeks, Robert P. "Fakery in *The Old Man and the Sea.*" *College English* 24 (December 1962):188–92. Reprinted in *Twentieth Century Interpretations of "The Old Man and the Sea,"* edited by Katharine T. Jobes, 34–40. Enumeration of details that diverge sharply from the realism of Hemingway's better work and elicit irreverent snickers toward *Old Man.*

Wells, Arvin R. "A Ritual of Transfiguration: *The Old Man and the Sea.*" *University Review* 30 (Winter 1963):95–101. Reprinted in *Twentieth Century Interpretations of "The Old Man and the Sea,"* edited by Katharine T. Jobes, 56–63. Analysis of religious symbolism that intermingles affirmation and guilt, redemption and destruction of life.

Wittkowski, Wolfgang. "Crucified in the Ring: Hemingway's *The Old Man and the Sea.*" *Deutsche Vierteljahrsschrift fur Literaturwissenschaft und Geistesgeschichte* (1967). Reprinted in *Hemingway Review* 3 (Fall 1983):2–17. Translated by Bonita Veysey and Larry Wells. Cogent reading of religious allusions to deny Santiago Christian status and to show his athlete's ethic.

Index

The Author

Gerry Brenner is a professor of English at the University of Montana, where he has taught for more than 20 years and where students voted him 1989's most inspirational teacher. Author of *Concealments in Hemingway's Works* (1983) and co-author with Earl Rovit of *Ernest Hemingway* (revised edition, 1986), he recently finished a three-year term as writer of the bibliographic essay on Fitzgerald and Hemingway for the annual reference volume *American Literary Scholarship*. In addition to essays on Hemingway, he has published critical articles on Chaucer, Shakespeare, Austen, Browning, Thoreau, Cooper, Twain, Fitzgerald, Hammett, Updike, Morrison, Flaubert, and Chekhov. A former Fulbright senior lecturer of American literature in Skopje, Yugoslavia, he is currently at work on two books—a glossary to Hemingway's *A Moveable Feast* and a collection of essays in fictive criticism.